*Journey to red birds*

*Journey to red birds*

Jan Lindblad

# *Journey to red birds*

TRANSLATED BY GWYNNE VEVERS

HILL AND WANG : NEW YORK

*Resa till röda fåglar* was first published in Sweden by Bonniers in 1966

Published in the United States of America by Hill and Wang, Inc.
Library of Congress catalog card number: 68-15871
First American Edition January 1969

Printed in Great Britain

*Contents*

## *Colour plates*

## *Black and white illustrations*

*To Camilla and Bobo*

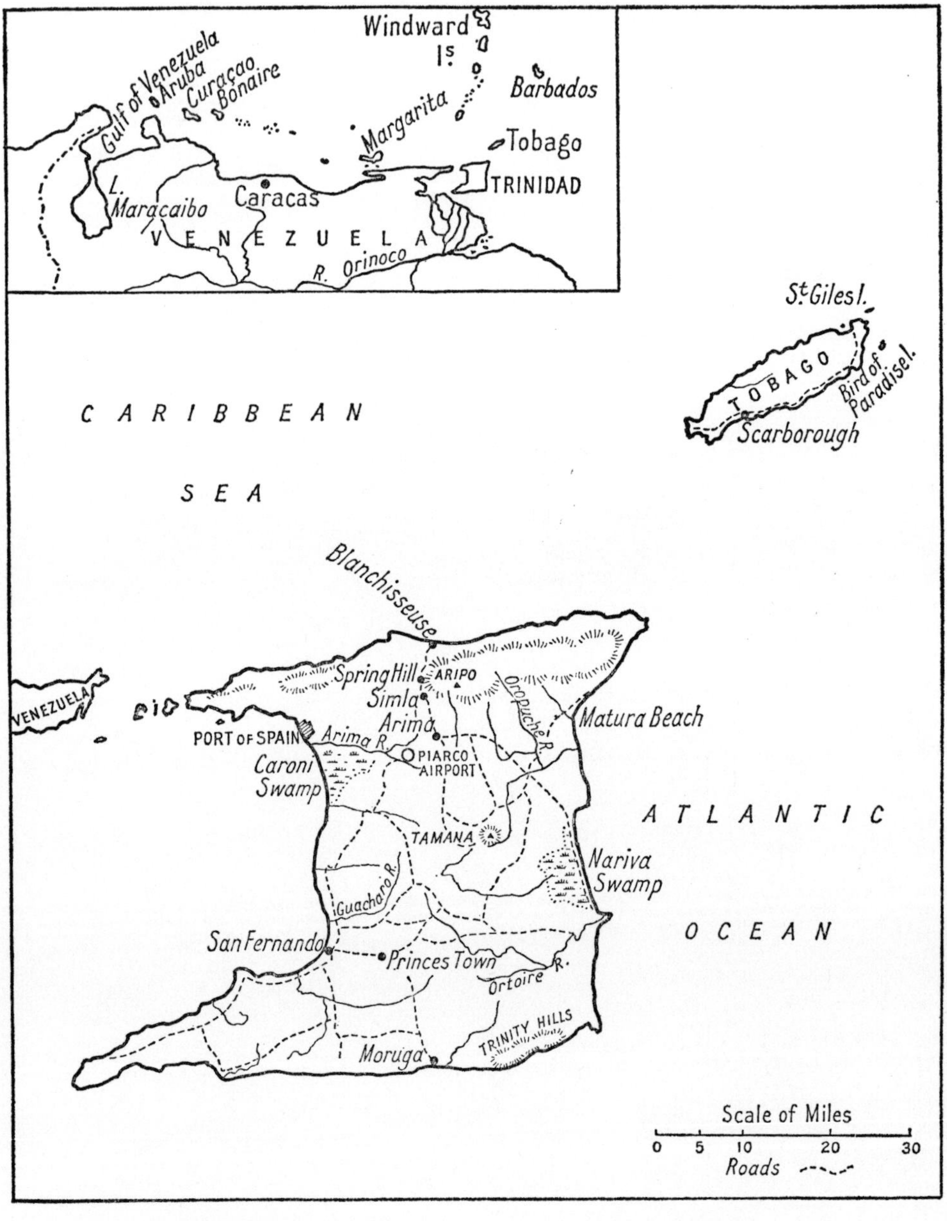


Trinidad and Tobago

# *Introduction*

The idea of going to the West Indies sprang from a chance remark made by my wife as we were driving along the road from Stockholm to our country cottage. The car was running smoothly and the landscape was aflame with colour in the autumn sunshine. We were in a happy mood because the day before my film, *Wild Country*, produced in collaboration with Swedish Films, had been awarded the 4th prize in the Swedish Film Institute's Diploma competition. The prize was worth about £12,000 ($33,600).

'I really think we can afford to travel a bit now and just enjoy ourselves,' said my wife. 'The winter is coming and you've been working hard on that wildlife film for six years. You should give yourself a little sunshine and warmth now. How about the West Indies?'

My wife's remarks merely served to encourage an idea which had started to germinate in my mind. It had been lying fallow too long and it was time I did something about it. I replied impulsively that it would be marvellous to have a look at the red ibises and flamingoes and of course I would be able to take my camera. I was as light-hearted about the decision as if it was as simple as going for a pleasant walk. That was how it all started. It was not the first time in my life that chance had led me to branch out along completely new lines. It reminded me of something which had happened when I was twelve years old. I saw a juggler performing who was an expert and at that age I was dazzled by his skill. I was so intrigued that I got hold of some old tennis balls and set to work. In the end I finished up in the lecture theatre at school performing a trick which involved throwing eight rings into the air and making a pyramid while balancing on a tightrope.

It was much the same kind of chance that made me take an interest in filming. It so happened that I had a lot of birds in my room when I noticed a film camera on display in a shop-window. It was an 8mm camera costing £16 ($44.80) . I knew very little about filming but I thought it would be fun to have some film of the birds before they flew away. At that time I was keeping about twenty birds in my room. I had bought them at various times during the winter. In spite of the prohibition on catching wild birds, various species were continually turning up in different pet-shops in Stockholm. There were nervous newly-caught robins, chaffinches, siskins, goldfinches, bullfinches, crossbills and others, fluttering about in small cages among canaries and budgerigars. I believed that they would do better in my room where I had brought branches of spruce, pine and juniper and covered the floor with a layer of moss.

On noticing the camera in the shop window I did not meditate outside for long but made up my mind quickly and went inside. I was soon persuaded by the salesman that another camera was better value and ended up by buying a secondhand 16mm camera for £43 ($120.40). The following week I exchanged this and found myself the possessor of a new, fully professional 16mm camera. My wallet was thinner but my head was full of glorious pictures.

The film of the birds in my room was of course useless, but during the following summer and for two further seasons I worked hard at my hobby and made three short films on the animal life of Sørmland. These were later used for film shows from which I financed the six-year project on the *Wild Country* in Dalecarlia.

In my experience, coincidence, lucky chance or passing fancy has always tended to develop into hard but enjoyable work. For months I filmed in different places in the West Indies. I travelled between Trinidad's forest-clad mountains and mangrove swamps, filming oilbirds at night, whirring hummingbirds and red clouds of ibis by day. I enjoyed the flamingoes at Bonaire and the frigate-birds around Tobago. In short I witnessed unique and colourful sights for the very first time. And all this came my way from a chance beginning.

# 1 *Tropical wilderness*

The trip intended as a holiday inevitably developed into something quite different. Having said that I would take my camera with me I ended up by taking a complete set of equipment which, when finally packed, weighed over four hundred pounds. This, of course, included pretty well everything that I thought I might need*.

Even the smallest item was of use at some time or other on my travels. With this equipment I was able to record visually and on sound most of the things I saw both above and below water in daylight, and now and again in the dark with the help of invisible infrared light. The only piece of equipment which was not used was the

* My basic equipment consisted of two Paillard cameras, with a series of lenses ranging from a wide-angle lens to one with a magnification of 24 times, two Hasselblads (a 500 C and a 1600 F), an Exakta, a Pentax, a Robot with accessories, and a Nagra tape-recorder. These were packed in cases lined with foam rubber. In addition I took a Paillard underwater casing for filming under water, an image intensifier which I had borrowed from a friend at Uppsala University, three battery-driven searchlights (a Sun-gun and two film lights), a parabolic sound reflector, and a particularly ingenious photo-cell gadget for automatic photography. The 16mm ciné film stock consisted of Kodachrome II and Tri-X, and later I obtained some infra-red film HIR 430. For the 6 × 6mm format I used Ektachrome Commercial and Ektachrome High Speed, Tri-X, and Verichrome Pan, and for the 35mm cameras Kodachrome II. I mention these details for people interested in photography.

photocell gadget. Thus none of the pictures in this book was taken automatically.

So the proposed holiday rapidly developed into a filming expedition. It was a one-man show to begin with, but my wife was to follow on as soon as she could. After a certain amount of thought I finally decided to try to see everything that was at all possible. I hoped to look through my viewfinder at red ibis, oilbirds, hummingbirds, flamingoes, fer-de-lance, anacondas and so on. I had been in touch with Swedish Radio and TV, and it was agreed that I should produce a series of films—a great stroke of luck, as it increased my resources considerably. My programme was almost entirely concerned with the West Indies. On my way out, I reflected that it was a somewhat longer expedition than my previous longest journey south—a return ferry trip from Helsingborg in south Sweden to Elsinore in Denmark.

In New York I obtained a quantity of some new ultra-fast 16mm film. The temperature in the city fluctuated around −20°C (−4°F). This was not exactly in line with the West Indian climate for which I was heading, but it was distinctly more suitable for the infra-red film, which is so sensitive to heat that it becomes fogged if it is not kept cool.

I took the opportunity to visit the American Museum of Natural History where I had the pleasure of meeting, among others, Professor Aronson and Dr Schneirla, who gave me much good advice about my journey and promised to get in touch with Dr Michael Emsley, the deputy director of the Simla Research Station. This is situated in the middle of Trinidad's sea of green rainforest; it was founded by the famous scientist and author William Beebe.

I therefore set my sights on Trinidad, the West Indian island with a South American flora and fauna—the land of hummingbirds as it is called. This was to be my first stop on a journey in which I planned to go right round South America. During the five hours' flight from New York the thermometer climbed from −20°C (−4°F) to +30°C

(86°F), and I landed in Trinidad wearing a heavy winter overcoat and a fur hat.

Next morning Michael Emsley flew me up to Simla in the mountains of Trinidad. Flew is the word, although in fact we used a car. Seven years on the roads of Trinidad had given Mike a death-defying technique from which Erik Carlsson and other rally-drivers could have learned a lot.

During my stay in Trinidad I learnt by experience that nothing is impossible for a Trinidad driver. An oncoming car will queue-jump shamelessly and lurch towards you on your side of the road, avoiding you by a hairbreadth. On occasions I was forced to drive right off the road because it was blocked by two lorries battling it out side by side, regardless of other traffic. Driving signals are mostly made by hand movements outside the window. These, however, are not to be relied upon, and only a trained psychologist with long experience of the behaviour of drivers in Trinidad could tell whether the hand-signals are the result of a driver discussing something with his passenger, moving his hands according to the state of the argument, or just giving his hand an airing when it gets too hot inside—or it could even mean that the driver intends to turn to the right or left. Also, as indicators are now beginning to become much more popular, hand-signals tend to disappear altogether on routine short journeys.

The car one hires is a hazard in itself. I called mine 'the rattlesnake' because it rattled and lurched from side to side. It was a dangerous machine with brakes that seized up, shiny smooth tyres, and indicators and headlights which did not work. I changed it four times and each time I was given 'the best car' according to all accounts. What the worst was like or how it ever functioned at all is anybody's guess. One of the roads in Trinidad is said to have the highest accident rate of any in the world, and a much-travelled man wrote in one of Trinidad's newspapers that the drivers there are the most inconsiderate in the world, more so even than Paris taxi-drivers.

As I said, we flew along the road to Simla. The roar of Mike's black Mercedes was well known and as we approached small villages on the road to Arima everyone got out of the way, for a tiger in the tank is no laughing matter. After a triumphal procession up Simla's own street we arrived providentially at the research station, where we were greeted by Mike's wife, Julie. Mike, who is principally an entomologist but also a very knowledgeable herpetologist, is fortunate in having a wife who is also a skilled colleague. Amongst other things Julie paints the colour plates which illustrate his scientific papers on regional variation in the wing patterns of certain butterflies. They are a busy couple who complement each other. They have already spent seven successful years in Trinidad.

William Beebe, the versatile zoologist who was interested in every living thing, fascinated the world with his accounts of scientific expeditions to such places as Venezuela and British Guiana. He is also known for his bathysphere dives to study deep-sea life at record depths. Surely it was not chance that led him to Simla and Trinidad? The island is a gold mine for a zoologist, just as for the photographer it offers an endless variety of subjects. I could not have chosen a better place in which to start an expedition for filming wildlife.

In Sweden I had been able to concentrate on the same subject in the same area year after year, fitting together the jigsaw puzzle of film sequences and gradually making them into a complete story. The compilation of material was a slow process—snail's pace compared with other film projects—but the only way to get results was by continually working and re-working the subject-matter, by trying new ways and discarding old ones, so as to learn all about the chosen theme.

***Trinidad's carnival is a two-day annual festival, a fiesta in all the colours of the rainbow accompanied by steel-band music which is the pride and joy of the local inhabitants.***

I soon realised that Trinidad's rich natural life presented not just a gigantic puzzle, but rather a series of ones. I stayed in Trinidad for a year, making trips to other areas for convenient periods but using the island as a base all the time. I had originally planned to build hides for the red ibises and in the caves of the oilbirds, and then to go off on a quick expedition through those areas of South America which interested me zoologically. I had to cover a lot of ground and in this way hoped to produce the requisite number of television programmes agreed upon with Swedish TV. Trinidad was therefore to have been the last stage and on the return journey I had planned to film the nesting ibises and oilbirds. This plan turned out not to be as simple as it sounded, but in the end I was glad because the revised schedule of work gave me the opportunity to follow up several animal species throughout a complete year, and this fitted in well with my methods.

I arrived just as the rainy season had ended and the forests were covered with red clouds of millions of immortelle blooms. Each day the colour tones, ranging between orange and warm red, gave me a feeling of happiness, but perhaps it was the fascination of hearing for the first time the music of the rain-forests that so captivated me. Nothing is more enjoyable than the chorus of sound which comes from a forest; each of these has its own musical score, be it the rich orchestra of a beechwood in Blekinge, the lonely quartet or quintet of a pine forest in Norrland, or the extravagant medley of tunes in Trinidad's rain-forests. Sounds have always fascinated me, for one hears much more than one sees, and this is particularly true in the labyrinths of luxuriant vegetation in the tropics.

To me nothing brings back the memory of a place so much as a

*The long, hanging nests of the yellowtail sway in the cool breeze amongst the flowers of a tall immortelle tree. These birds are characteristic of the mountain districts of Trinidad and their penetrating notes carry far in the rain-forest.*

sound remembered. I can recall sounds so vividly that if I shut my eyes I can see the place in my mind all over again, and hear the forest orchestra once more playing. A series of deep, gentle tones like the beat in the lowest register of a marimba means a trogon, coloured blue, yellow and green—a fine musical background to the slow, melancholy, but sonorous tones of a white-throated thrush, the Pan of the rain-forest. Toucans fly through the tree-tops with harsh calls, which put everything on the alert. The sound of a bellbird is so incredibly loud that it is as though the bird were tapping an iron girder. It almost completely drowns the little flock of humming-birds, which weave their delicate pattern of voices in a gossamer of treble squeaks. Amongst it all one can hear the volley of sharp cracks made by the black-and-white manakins, which signal with pistol shots when a female turns up at the display place. All these sounds encourage the listener to delve further into the life-histories of the various species.

Trinidad is by no means just rain-forest. On the contrary it resembles rather tropical South America in miniature, with its different types of terrain: savannah, marshes and forest of various kinds, culminating in the highest mountains in the northern part of the island. This is a continuation of the mountain chain in the neighbouring part of Venezuela. Trinidad had quite a recent land connection with the mainland, hence the similarity of its fauna to that of Venezuela. Geographically and zoogeographically it is more correct to compare the island with South America than with the other West Indian islands, which share most of their fauna with the southern parts of North America.

Trinidad is the most southerly of the West Indian islands and the largest of the Lesser Antilles. In spite of this it covers only 2,000 square miles. The climate is a healthy tropical one with an average temperature fluctuating between 25° and 30°C (77°-86°F). The rainfall is dependent upon the north-east trade-winds; the amount of rain is greatest along the north coast and the annual rainfall at different places varies from 47 to 150 inches. Most rain falls during

August; the period from January to May is called the dry season but there is a good deal of heavy rain, especially in the mountain districts. In my opinion this is just right; it means a lovely damp warm atmosphere in the mountains, which surely provides the best living conditions in the world for *Homo sapiens*.

From the northern mountain range, with Aripo (940m, 3,085 feet) and El Tucuche (936m, 3,071 feet) as the highest peaks, the amount of rain decreases but gathers here and there in the swampy areas. The larger of these areas are connected to the sea and the water is partially brackish. On the east coast lies Nariva, which is an eldorado for plants and mosquitoes. It is also the place where one can see the big blue-and-yellow macaw and its relative the scarlet macaw. The Bush-Bush research station, where special investigations are made on the spread of yellow fever by insects and mammals, is situated in this area. Caroni Swamp is a marshy area on the west coast, which is the home of the scarlet ibis; in the past Oropuche Swamp and Cedros Swamp were also visited by this species, which has recently been designated the national bird of Trinidad.

In addition to the northern mountains which give distinctive character and dimension to the landscape, there is a range of low hills in the centre of the island, about 900 feet high, and a similar formation on the coast in the south with three peaks known as Trinity Hills. It was from this side in 1498 that Columbus, on his third voyage, looked out to discover the island; he saw the three peaks and decided to name them after the Holy Trinity. Hence Trinidad's name.

At this time the island was inhabited by several Indian peoples, of which the Arawaks in the south-east and the Caribs in the north and west were the two most important. The visit of the Spaniards passed off without any trouble; they had the luck to meet the Arawaks, whom Columbus found to be charming and friendly people. Had he met the Caribs, in the area where the present capital city Port of Spain lies, the meeting would scarcely have been an amicable one. The name Carib has given rise to the word cannibal, and indicates a good deal about the social habits of these people. When Columbus reached the island of Dominica, he annexed the area in the name of Spain but had to break off his stay on account of a rain of arrows.

Almost pure-blooded Caribs are still found in Arima (which means water in the Carib language), but they are numerically an insignificant minority. Trinidad's present-day population is perhaps the most heterogeneous in the world with strains from all parts of the globe. The Spaniards were the first European element, but in 1783 so many French arrived that they soon out-numbered them. This might have meant the area becoming a French possession, but instead it was the British who occupied Trinidad in 1797, although it did not become a British Crown Colony until the Peace of Amiens in 1802. In 1962, Trinidad and Tobago finally became independent.

The European element is, however, by no means restricted to the Spaniards, French and British. Early on there came Portuguese, Italians, Germans and Swiss. Today the whites form only about 3% of the total population. At least 47% are Negroes, descendants of the slaves who were brought in from West Africa, in themselves an extremely complex population and representative of many people: Yoruba, Hausa, Ibo, Ashanti, Arada and so on.

When slavery was abolished throughout the British Empire in 1834, the plantation owners were left with a major labour problem. In this strained situation the frontiers were opened to an enormous wave of immigrating Indians, whose descendants now make up 35% of the population. The Chinese, who constitute 1%, had also moved in earlier under the same conditions, as contract workers. All these population elements have been added to from various quarters and there has been a lot of interbreeding. The result is a mixture of races such as is found in few other parts of the world.

Many of the people one sees in Port of Spain are extremely attractive, showing traces of both eastern and western ancestry. A woman with the slanting eyes of a Chinese, the smiling expression of an Indian, the grace and elegance of a Frenchwoman, together with perhaps a little American Indian blood, can be extremely fascinating. Perhaps it is also this rich mixture of races which is responsible for the fabulous variety which can be seen at Trinidad's well-known carnival, where the spectacular fancy-dress gala makes the stories from *A Thousand and One Nights* appear but pale shadows. It is a Cinderella-like saga which does not end on the stroke of twelve but goes on for two whole days and nights, forty-eight hours of a hectic, fantastic experience.

The houses on the outskirts of Port of Spain are indescribably poor; the material used for the walls varies from corrugated iron to rotten boards and cardboard. In spite of this, in the period before the carnival many of these hovels are decorated with ostrich plumes, and the walls shine and glitter with tinsel and paste. The dresses seen during carnival time are so full of fantasy that one might think the island had been invaded by people from a friendly planet. In the centre of Port of Spain lies Queen Park Savannah where a gigantic platform is constructed; during the two days one procession after another goes past. There seem to be hundreds and hundreds of people taking part. I tried to find out exactly how many, but nobody knew; it is impossible to attempt even an estimate of the numbers of people on a platform six hundred feet long which is full of an endless stream of gay and dancing bodies. Each group has a common theme. For instance, a north American Indian tribe with men and women painted in full war-paint carry their wigwams with them. An African tribe struggles along with a complete palisade of decapitated heads of lions and white men. They dance in a leaping, seething mass and then suddenly all fall into the rhythm of the accompanying steel-band. Soon everyone imagines himself transplanted to the real Africa. One group is dressed up as a lot of American soldiers who suddenly open fire on each other with death-leaps and a clamour worthy of a stunt on a film-set. In the middle of the crowd a group of Vikings appear in thick furs, with a long table stacked with meat and food. The drama of *A Thousand and One Nights*, Incas and everything that one can possibly think of is found in the parade. It continues for so long that one would never dream of standing in the burning sun were it not for the scene constantly changing like a living kaleidoscope.

The only thing that is monotonous is the music, in which the same tunes are played with few variations. Steel-band after steel-band marches past the platform, with a deep cacophony from the ping-pong pans topping the boom from the bass, the tempo marked with the jingle of brake drums and other parts of scrap cars. And as the day proceeds the music gets more and more out of tune, the heat of the sun and the continuous beating causing the metal to change shape. One might think that after three hours of musical execution it would be wise to tune the instruments, but no one is willing to miss a second of the two days' festivities.

Apart from this, it is astonishing how fine a musical performance can be given on something that was previously an oil-drum. I have heard Debussy's 'Clair de Lune' quite clearly on a ping-pong pan and it is said that even Beethoven's Fifth Symphony has been so played. On the day after peace was declared in 1945, the people of Trinidad held their own celebrations. For five years they had been forbidden to hold carnivals; all their pent-up feelings broke loose and the old instruments of bamboo, unable to stand up to the continual thumping, fell to bits. The bamboo was dead but long live the metal! Everything that jingled and clanged, thundered and banged, helped to make a chaos of sound. In the relatively short time since the birth of this oil-drum music, an enormous amount of petrol has been refined in Trinidad, accompanied by a considerable development in petrol drums. Boom pans have four tones, cello pans five or six, guitar pans fourteen and ping-pong pans up to thirty-two.

The music may have changed but it will take a good deal longer for the musicians to change. Certainly at the last carnival everything was thought to have gone off well, the result after two days being only two dead and some sixty injured. In the past some steel-band musicians have been feared for their wild temperament and their habit of taking a rest from the thumping of the oil-drum by grabbing their razors and poi-yahs, knives or cutlasses. Today the atmosphere is somewhat calmer, perhaps due to the influence of the words of the well-known calypso song:

> Too many gangs and too much slash
> Too many daggers and cutlass
> Too many reach the hospital
> Too many people end up in funeral
> What is the reason for all this
> Cut out this blinking foolishness
> Jump in the crowd and play the mas
> But don't bring no razor or cutlass.

Violence is most marked in Port of Spain because of the many social anomalies there, but the same tendency to settle an argument by force is found all over the island, in big and small gatherings. For example, at a dance in St Joseph's some youths who were denied entrance returned later with razors. Eleven of the lucky ones who had gained admittance were slashed. When a couple of my friends got married it was considered completely natural for them to engage police to prevent any such incidents. In a fracas at a factory in Arima two men fought so bitterly that they were taken to hospital and the police were called. 'Only a bit of fun,' they declared. One of them had the whole of his back ripped by a razor.

There was a case of violence near Simla, while I was living there, in which a man had the tops of his fingers on one hand cut off by a machete when trying to ward off a blow. Some days later when I was driving to Arima I saw the man who had delivered the blow and offered him a lift. Later I asked whether he had really intended to strike his opponent through the neck, as this seemed to be the general opinion. He looked mortally offended and pointed out that he would have done so had he wished. No, they had both been arguing, a little energetically perhaps, gesticulating and talking with their hands—and he had happened to be holding his cutlass in his right hand!

There is no doubt that life in Trinidad appears to be pretty chaotic. One of the reasons given for this is that the new Constitution is still so young. Life was affected in various ways by independence and as far as I was concerned the worst repercussions came when I had to deal with the Customs. My fourteen cases of film equipment were naturally detained but it took three days of rushing back and forth between different offices in Port of Spain before I could collect everything together and get it out of the airport premises at Piarco. At first they wanted a deposit of over £1,000 ($2,800). Each time I went on my travels, there were similar incidents. This has never happened to me in other countries where the Customs arrangements are more flexible.

Otherwise I was treated with friendliness and helpfulness by everyone I met on the island. Among others, I soon made friends with Don Eckelberry, the well-known illustrator of *Birds of the West Indies*. His studies are so life-like that each bird looks on the point of flying off the page. For some years now Don has regarded the island of Trinidad, and its more than four hundred avian species, as a gift from heaven. The island's resident ornithologist *par excellence* is Richard Ffrench, who takes all available time off from his job as a teacher to watch and ring birds, accompanied by his wife Margaret. I am grateful to all three for their friendly help in giving me an overall picture of the island's birds in such a relatively short space of time.

Simla gradually filled up with research workers from various parts of the world, including the United States, Britain, Germany, and Japan. Eventually even Dr Jocelyn Crane, Director of the Research Station, arrived back after her world-tour studying fiddler-crabs.

I eventually stayed six weeks in Simla. Instead of a fleeting acquaintance with Trinidad on the first stage of my journey, I stayed on for a whole year and fell in love with it.

The island with its rich animal world offers so much within so small an area that I felt as though I had met the tropical equivalent of my home ground in the Dalecarlia district of Sweden. Also the northern mountain range reminded me so much of the landscape that I had only to half-close my eyes to imagine that instead of the mile upon mile of rain-forest, I was looking once again at the outlines of the eagle owl mountains.

# 2 *A study in blood-red*

Caroni Swamp on the west coast of Trinidad is an eldorado for huge numbers of birds, including both breeding species and winter visitors from the north. The River Caroni carries with it a mud that is rich in nutriment. This mud reaches a depth of several yards in a big area of marsh where the jumble of mangrove is broken up by open channels of water. At high tide the mud-banks are covered to a depth of about three feet with black, turbid water; at low tide the whole area is left dry except for a network of runnels. It is as well to be familiar with these when navigating in this 'sea of blackness'. When the water has receded the greyish-black mud swarms with crabs and small organisms that are an epicurean delicatessen for hungry birds. Amongst others a varied assortment of herons thrive, which are beautiful from the point of view both of shape and colour. Nevertheless they are completely overshadowed by one species—the red ibis. This handsome bird, which might have been designed for colour photography, was the main reason why I chose Trinidad as the first stopping-place on my journey. It was also responsible for my staying a whole year on the island, with only relatively short trips to other areas.

Transport to Caroni presented certain problems but these were solved with the assistance of a young Indian named Winston Nanan. He and his family act as guides for the steadily increasing stream of tourists who wish either to sample the rich fishing or to admire the bird life. Winston is an experienced bird-watcher who is very interested in photography. In addition he is something very rare in

Trinidad—considerate and careful when it comes to anything to do with wild life.

I was very excited by the prospect of seeing the scarlet ibis, this brilliant red member of Trinidad's bird fauna. I still had to get my equipment through the Customs, a procedure which involved a confusion of paper work and the payment of £300 ($840), and which lasted three whole days in the broiling heat of Port of Spain. The route to Caroni passes through the shadowy darkness of the mangroves and out over water-courses where the sun pours down overhead; it follows the network of drainage channels that are invisible under the black water. As we made our way along the channels, a snowy egret flew up ahead, and a little farther on a little blue heron floundered about as it made its way ahead of the boat through the long green tunnels. The journey was punctuated with bizarre sounds: there were bursts of scornful laughter from a species of ant-shrike, some knife-sharp cries from night herons taken by surprise, and the raucous call of a tricoloured heron. A flash of green and a kingfisher, very like the European one but even smaller, followed us through a narrow channel; it was so near that a bird-ringer could almost have caught it. Its call reminded me of our own kingfisher at home. Then I heard another sharp high-pitched call coming from directly overhead. To people who are not familiar with it this whistling note suggests a small bird, but when I heard it I felt I was back in Sweden again. I waited for the curtain of mangroves to part and there it was high overhead—an osprey, just as it looked one day at Bäven in Sørmland.

The fauna at home seems drab-coloured indeed when compared to the violent contrasts of the tropics. My first sight of the ibises was like the outburst of a tropical storm after a long period of oppressive calm. A crescendo of wings, the sound burst forth like the buffeting of blows in a battle, and a flood of blood-red ibises poured out in a seemingly endless flow over the water in the channels. The visual impact was stupendous. The beauty of the scarlet ibis surpasses all others in the bird world. Initially I felt stunned, but this was only the beginning of a growing sense of wonder which gradually became refined into the absolute quintessence of ornithological delight. As I write this, I have now had the advantage of seeing this living flame of fire for almost a whole year under a great variety of conditions from a score of photographic viewpoints. About twenty hours' running time of ciné-film and masses of still photographs have been used up in an attempt to do justice to the brilliant glow of colour which comes from the wings. Every evening after a day in the broiling sun at Caroni, I was left almost groaning with pleasure from feasting on such richness.

Many of the birds in these tropical latitudes have boldly contrasting colours in their plumage. They are like an artist's palette with gaudy hues side by side, almost monotonous in their showiness. I found, however, that my eyes were never tired by the sight of the scarlet ibis. The red feather guise is all of a piece, like the scarlet cloak of a Roman general, artistically uniform except for the four outermost wing primaries, which are dipped in black. The black areas are actually iridescent green, like the overall plumage of the glossy ibis, and the birds glow like freshly oxygenated blood when seen under the first slanting rays of the morning sun. As the ibises gather in open flocks over the dark waters, it is as though they are burning with their own inner light. In the late evening as hundreds and thousands of them cascade down to the marsh there is a murmuration of sound under the reddening skies.

In August, 1965, there were more than 7,000 of these birds at Caroni. When I saw them in such profusion I found it difficult to remember that the scarlet ibis is in fact very rare—a species that is uncomfortably close to extinction. Lying at the root of this paradox, as usual, is the despoliation of the countryside by modern man. During the latter half of the nineteenth century these red birds were reported to be extremely numerous in all the mangrove areas of the coastal regions of South America, from Colombia through Venezuela and Guyana to northern Brazil.

With the arrival of motor-boats and automatic weapons, both

transport and shooting became a practical proposition. These modern techniques made it possible for man to indulge his lust for hunting, and with no restrictions to check man's thirst for blood the survival of the scarlet ibis was swiftly endangered. The result of fifty to sixty years of destruction is both upsetting and frightening: a flagrant example of the war of extermination carried on by *Homo sapiens*, consciously or unconsciously, against other species of animal.

In 1949, Dr Paul A. Zahl started to organise an expedition to Venezuela to look for the scarlet ibis. He had sent out a 'scout' the year before to make a thorough search of localities where the species was most likely still to be found. At one time the main stronghold of the ibis was Venezuela, and it was anything but rare in the extensive delta system of the Orinoco. The search during these two years resulted in the finding of only one colony of scarlet ibis. This was more than four hundred miles from the mouth of the Orinoco in an area between the tributaries Apure and Matillure. The coastal regions with their salty mud, rich in crustaceans, are the natural habitat of the species, and evidence of its disappearance was very apparent. From the pictures which Dr Zahl published in the *National Geographic Magazine* one can in fact read the evidence of the fading colour of the bird from scarlet to almost pink. In the accompanying article he described how he had examined the stomach contents of many of the birds and found plant material but no trace of the animal food which is the standard diet of the deep red ibis of Trinidad. It is clear that diet, especially the diet of crustaceans, is of importance for the deposition of the red pigment in the growing feathers. A red ibis gradually becomes pale pink in captivity. Now and again the ibises in Port of Spain Zoo, about twelve miles from Caroni, have all had this sickly pallor.

On the journey through Georgetown in Guyana I asked the Museum Superintendent, Ram Singh, whether the birds were still breeding there. The answer was in the negative, for no colony had been found within the country's boundaries for several years. The ibises which are now found at Caroni suddenly arrived there in 1953.

This was ten years after the birds had been driven from the island by the same irresponsible persecution as had taken place on the mainland. The authorities realised the importance of this invasion. The area occupied by the ibises was quickly declared a prohibited one and a very successful breeding season followed. All was well. Here the birds had a chance to increase in peace and quiet, protected from man in an area where no other predators threatened. There were no birds of prey or owls to take toll of the population, and rich food, especially crustaceans and small organisms, was present in abundance.

I had originally thought of building photographic hides in strategic positions near suitable breeding trees, well before the nesting season, so that I could get on with my plans for touring South America and then return to the scarlet ibises, when I received word that the birds had started to nest. This, however, was not so easy. I inquired when it would be safe to assume that the birds had hatched their young. To my astonishment I learnt that nobody knew. It had been more than two years since they had started to build and then the breeding was not completely successful because the birds were not left in peace.

With increasing dismay I learned something which seemed completely incredible: the ibis, Trinidad's national bird and as such legally protected, was in practice not protected at all. During the previous two years every suggestion of an attempt at breeding had failed owing to poachers, who naturally found it was convenient to hunt in a restricted and protected area at a time when masses of birds were assembling in readiness for breeding. As it happened, it was not long before I had direct evidence of the truth of these stories.

Winston and I frequently went out at 4 o'clock in the morning from our anchorage, which lay in a channel conveniently near to our Land-Rover. Cameras, tape-recorders, parabolic reflector and other equipment were loaded in the darkness, while frogs and toads played their ceaseless, many-voiced concert—a music which degrades the latest modern electronic composition to third-class status. We chugged along the channels, where red cats' eyes shone brightly and disappeared twenty yards away; the caymans thrive here in the continual fresh water. Every so often the same red eyes appeared to be suspended from a broken-off bamboo stem close to the channel. If one cuts off the motor and shines a light, the upper part of the bamboo turns out to be a bird. A potoo or giant nightjar sits tight until we are four to five yards from it. Then the orange-red cat's eyes, glowing in the darkness a foot above the bamboo stem, fly off as the bird takes wing.

When we come out into the sea of blackness and approach the birds' night quarters, Winston takes the long punt-pole. Silently we glide through the water, breaking up the reflection of stars. The potoo starts to wail and some Cayenne woodrails follow with a ping-pong contest of softly echoing sounds. It becomes light quickly and birds begin to move. We see the long line of birds gliding forward over the tops of the mangroves and watch where they go to feed so that we can work out where best to get close-ups later in the day. It seems as though the birds change their feeding areas by chance. Sometimes some particular banks will be popular, at other times these are completely neglected even though they are crawling with crustaceans.

The birds are mostly moving northwards today, choosing the banks perhaps in the little bay which was so crammed full of crabs yesterday. The tide is coming in and by 11 o'clock it is high tide and the birds move into the tangle of mangroves. By 3 o'clock the banks ought to be sufficiently dried out again. With luck the birds will be there at 4 o'clock and there should be good light from the west. When the tidal water is highest we start to move out, for there are then no birds to scare away.

The red ibises proved to be extremely shy, on the alert for every sign of danger. The poachers are silent when they move into position on some well-stocked mud-bank; here there may be four to five hundred birds wandering about, like red blooms waiting to be picked off with shot-guns or automatic guns. One may well ask why the scarlet ibis should be so highly prized. For one thing it tastes good. As an official in Port of Spain said to me, with a somewhat rueful laugh: 'The national bird has indeed become our national dish.'

Its most eye-catching characteristic, the red plumage, is conceivably a contributory factor. At carnival time when everyone is brimming over with high spirits, the supply of red feathers for decorative purposes needs to be almost inexhaustible. In addition, it could be that some taxidermist is responsible for part of the slaughter. Such things have been known in Sweden in spite of the protection of nature. A finely mounted red ibis should have considerable value, particularly in view of its rarity nowadays.

We had plenty of opportunity to hear the poachers at work. Now and then during the day a cannonade would rend the air some distance away. The guns were particularly active at sunset when the flocks moved quickly back towards their night quarters, which also lie in the protected area, ironically known as the Sanctuary. We often met the corpses of dead birds caught in tree branches or floating among the roots of the mangroves. The sight of such perfect beauty being wantonly destroyed made me increasingly angry.

When I go out hunting I take nothing except my cameras. The poachers at Caroni do not come in the category of the destitute, for someone who has an automatic gun and a 20-horse-power Johnson motor cannot be described as such and should have plenty of opportunities for making a living in other ways. I found this illegal form of hunting, with its wanton slaughter, completely nauseating.

I never saw the game wardens who should have been keeping the poachers away and who, incidentally, should have checked my permit to visit the protected area. I wondered to whom I should go to put a stop to the unrestricted harrying of the birds. I referred the matter to Mike Emsley. Although not employed as a game warden,

ABOVE *The roseate spoonbill is a colourful but rare visitor to the bird marshes of Trinidad. This species has not yet bred on the island.* BELOW *Three versions of the tricoloured heron: as a shadow, as a reflection, and as a highly efficient fishing expert. The thin down on this young heron's crown is still visible.*

he is recognised as such and given the honorary title as a well-known zoologist with seven years' experience in Trinidad. When I suggested to him that perhaps he might take some action, he replied with a shrug of his shoulders:

'The poachers are quick on the draw if surprised, and even if I managed to turn them over to the law my intervention would be fatal for Simla. Some night the buildings would simply catch fire. I have my family to think about. Sorry, but it's out of the question.'

Mike knew what he was talking about. During the following year a man who undertook to assassinate another for the sum of twenty shillings was caught and convicted. Life is cheap in Trinidad—even human life.

ABOVE *Scarlet ibises on the wing.* BELOW *Some of the mudflats are extremely popular on certain days. Birds assemble on the flats to feed on the fiddler-crabs in the mud. Scarlet ibises and little blue herons, including the young which are still in their white plumage, enjoy these delicacies. The small birds in the foreground are lesser yellowlegs.*

J.R.B.

# 3 *'Protected' area*

The filming at Caroni continued and Winston and I were out every day that was fine. It was completely out of the question, however, to film the ibis during the breeding season. Instead, I devoted myself to recording on film as many as possible of the day-to-day hunting and fishing activities of the egrets and other birds on the mud-banks.

In the mornings, when we had worked out roughly where the crab feast would take place, we went to the location and found a suitable mangrove bush. Here we pushed the boat into the mangroves and camouflaged its sides and also the camera with sacking daubed with green and black. To complete the camouflage we also cut off branches and stuck them around us in the mud. We then settled down to wait.

More often than not nothing happened. The terrain at Caroni is extensive and the birds capricious. Flocks of small waders—lesser yellowlegs which are closely related to the redshank and greenshank of Europe—crowded around everywhere and were reflected in the shallow pools of water on the mud-banks. As I watched these small, elegant waders making holes in the surface of the water with their pointed bills, I was reminded of Narcissus—the mythical being who tried to kiss his own reflection.

Waiting for birds is never monotonous. Often from small events on the periphery one collects unexpected information about the birds one is watching or about completely different animals. This chance information helps to clarify behaviour patterns and the relationship of animals to their environment. To pass the time there were the ever-present little fiddler-crabs. These have one claw shaped remarkably like a fiddle or violin and one wonders why such a small crab should have such a big claw. It is only the males which are equipped with this powerful pincer. It is an effective tool, sharp enough perhaps for cutting copper wire, or so I judged one day after getting a nasty shock through putting my little toe among the legs of an angry specimen lying in the bottom of the boat.

When all the males start running around and waving their 'hands' in the air, it reminds me of my year in the opera ballet school. The whole mudflat seems to be waving, as though the breeze were rippling amongst lots of small brown plants. The total effect is so graceful and the behaviour of the crabs so fascinating that when an egret appears it is almost an unwelcome intrusion, even though it is the object of the day's filming. It becomes particularly exciting when two of the crabs decide to have a proper battle. They move closer to each other with their eyes literally on stalks. While this is going on, the other claw, which is small and like a pair of forceps, continues to grope for small organisms on the surface of the mud.

The two contestants adopt a rigid stance and the affair is rapidly settled with the same swiftness and elegance as a judo demonstration. The claws clash together, like the clinking handshake between knights of old, and the loser is turned over, armour and all. Nothing more happens except that the loser retires from the scene at a quick trot, exposing its unprotected rear to the victor. This may seem strange but perhaps is equivalent to the behaviour of a vanquished wolf, which offers its unprotected neck to the winner as a sign of submission, and is not then attacked again.

Dr Jocelyn Crane, the Director of Simla, is particularly interested in these small animals. When I was there, she had just undertaken a circumtropical journey in order to study variations in the behaviour patterns of different races. I can well understand that a detailed study of their behaviour is worth all this time and effort.

One afternoon we were particularly lucky as the area of mudflat we had selected turned out to be the place where certain fastidious feeders chose to meet for a meal. As we lay in wait, watching the sunlit arena surrounded by high clumps of mangrove, some little blue herons came gliding in. There were dark blue adults and white juveniles. The crabs disappeared as if by magic. The herons landed and stiffened like statues, the typical posture of a heron on the hunt for food. Any self-respecting heron should be able to stand in the same position for several minutes. Something moved down in the narrow crab hole and the heron's pointed bill scarcely seemed to move as it got into position. As the crab came up, it was caught with a quick snap of the bill. The heron shifted its grip a couple of times and the titbit slid slowly through the long oesophagus, clearly visible as a lump going down the heron's neck.

After half an hour there was a promising murmur high up above us, which died down only to increase again after a time, and we recognised a flock of ibises approaching cautiously. Everything went well and the flock spread out and came in to land amongst the blue herons. The picture was complete: blue, white and glowing red, like a tricolor.

Completely absorbed by the combination of colours, I worked away with my film camera. Winston, who had borrowed one of my still cameras with a 600mm telephoto lens, took one picture after another. At the back of my mind I was aware that neither the sound of the film running nor the hard click of the shutter seemed to have any disturbing effect on the birds at Caroni. Everywhere there were insects humming, and at ebb-tide masses of oysters that sat attached to the mangrove roots closed their shells with a noise which would have made a Hasselblad 1000 F turn green with envy.

When one is accustomed to listening with concentration one can distinguish fine variations among all the general noise. On this occasion I suddenly heard something that did not belong to the normal pattern of sound. I tried to make out what it could be and decided it was not one mangrove branch rubbing against another in the gentle breeze. I listened again and then realised what it was. I put my hand on Winston's shoulder and my finger to my lips. We listened intently. The sound came again and it was that of a long mangrove pole grazing against a boat-rail. It could only be poachers sneaking up towards their prey, the group of ibis. The sound approached incredibly slowly as the boat came through the same narrow channel which we ourselves had used earlier.

I glanced at the camera. There was almost half a roll left. That should be enough to film them red-handed. After the shooting they would have to come closer and step out onto the grey expanse. The mud would hold them fast and the camera lens would also capture them. I realised that Winston's thoughts were running along the same lines. We had a chance to get enough pictorial evidence, both film and stills, to have them locked up.

The boat came closer and closer. Finally only a wall of about ten to twelve yards of mangrove separated us. Suddenly another flock of ibis came sweeping in, making the same manœuvre as the first, but these rose almost at once, giving their nasal alarm call. The birds out on the mud stretched their necks, spied out the land and listened. All at once the whole flock took off. Not a word was spoken by the men in the mangrove channel, but after a time there was a splash and a thud as the boat was carelessly punted back. In spite of the fact that we had lost the chance of recording the poachers in the act, I was glad. To have seen the birds shot would have been a revolting experience.

One evening some days later there was another chance. We found ourselves in front of a typical roosting tree of the ibises, properly hidden behind mangrove and camouflage sacking. The evening was fine and we ate our sandwiches and had a drink from the ice-box, enjoying the relative coolness after the heat of the sun during the day. In another twenty minutes the sun would be setting.

As though by a dispensation of nature, the red ibises move to the trees where they will spend the night at the very time when the light is saturated with red from the setting sun. The clear, cloudless evening sky suddenly glows with red, the wind whistles through hundreds of feathers as a flock comes in fast with powerful wing-beats to stop suddenly, as if at a word of command, and glide silently on, their outlines etched against the darkening sky. A muffled murmur of wings momentarily caresses the twilight before they flutter down into the soft green mangroves.

The birds continue to come in closely packed, weighing down the branches, fluttering and squabbling over roosting places. The short, nasal calls blend with the sound of wings brushing against the foliage of the branches and making crackling sounds as the dry twigs break. The steady stream of sound is like the crackling of a bonfire. There is an overall impression of fire: the fluttering red shapes leap like flames to the accompaniment of the breaking of dry twigs.

A passage from the second book of Moses comes to my mind, where Moses thinks he hears the voice of God speaking to him out of a burning bush. It suddenly occurs to me that the natural explanation might lie here. I begin to play with the idea in my mind: just as the glossy ibis has wandered to South America from Europe or Africa in recent times, so in bygone days might it not have been possible for a flock of the enormously numerous scarlet ibis to have flown across the Atlantic in the opposite direction? The sight that I am now looking at is so awe-inspiring that the ancient Egyptians, for example, would surely have taken it as a sign from the gods and declared the birds sacred. Three species of ibis occur in hieroglyphics, but just what these species are is not very easily determined. Another thought strikes me. In ancient times this form of protection was extremely effective. Who would dare to draw the wrath of the gods on himself by molesting a sacred bird?

As my thoughts continue to wander we hear shots. They come as a warning that a new flock is on the way. Every burst of shot is followed punctually by a wave of birds. The last rays of the sun leave the highest tree-tops, the clouds above light up the scene with a gentle, diffuse but still quite strong light. The birds are now almost self-illuminating, as though they are carrying red side-lights. Two thousand ibises, perhaps more, decorate the trees in front of us, making them look as though they were laden with red blooms.

Once again we hear the feeble thump of a pole against the side of a boat. The poachers are moving slowly into shooting range. Slowly they come on, closer and closer. Then, with a rush of wings, the whole enormous bouquet of roses explodes into the sky and fills it with thousands of fluttering petals, leaving the tree as if caught by a powerful gust of wind. Rocking and swaying in a column above the tree, the flock hangs in the sky, and then moves off.

As the noise of the vast murmur of wings dies away, the engine in the motor-boat starts up. We have heard no more shots, for there must have been some clumps of trees in the way. Out on the water a boat with five poachers moves off. Unfortunately the film camera was fitted with a telephoto lens directed towards the tree. It was impossible to tilt it down towards the water surface, as it was tucked in amongst the camouflage netting and branches, but I signalled to Winston. As usual he had borrowed one of my cameras. He focused and pressed the button. The light was good, the boat was close enough to fill the picture: five figures, four of them equipped with cartridge belts and with guns at the ready. What a picture, what a brilliant piece of evidence against them! Our jubilation lasted for only a quarter of an hour, for when I started to unload the camera I realised we had completely forgotten to put any film in.

The blackness closed in around us: the night was black, the mud was black. As we pushed our boat yard by yard through the viscous mass, splashing through it on the ebb, the mud of Caroni had never felt so heavy, so irritating to the skin and so evil-smelling. We continued filming at the same place as before, and without doubt our secret operation, with its twofold aim of watching the birds and trying to obtain pictorial evidence against the poachers, now became really exciting. The golden chance we had been given was not repeated but although we did not get any pictures something else happened.

One evening we found ourselves very close to a communal roosting tree. Cattle egrets and snowy egrets came down in droves and the tree looked veritably laden with snow as the screaming birds settled in. This snowstorm stood out well against the blue background of

Trinidad's mountains. A large flock of ibis made a beautiful contrast to all the whiteness as they arrived on the side of the tree which faced our hide. While operating the tape-recorder I enjoyed the sight of the bright red spots, which slowly lost their fire. The parabolic reflector picked up the grunting notes remarkably well in addition to other notes characteristic of the individual species.

As the skies darken, everything seems to lose its definition for a while. Then the light of the half-moon takes over. The white herons become pale blue. Carefully we glide out from our hide, a small mangrove bush about 75 yards from the birds. The tide is coming in and this suits us. Later on during the evening we should be able to punt out to the deeper tidal channels.

I hear some whistling sounds made by a duck: the fulvous tree-duck, a species seldom seen here but which I filmed in their hundreds yesterday. The sound needs recording to back up the film. I get out the parabolic reflector, microphone, tape-recorder and earphones. I direct the reflector towards the whistling and the usual thing happens. After a few seconds the birds become silent. With earphones on and volume full up, I listen while sweeping the horizon with the parabolic reflector.

A potoo can be heard quite distinctly although it is a few miles away. Some degrees farther round there is an ahoyo or white-naped nightjar with a Spix's screech owl and when I turn the parabolic still farther round I can hear the aeroplanes at Piarco warming up—but there is also something else. A motor-boat makes a cautious approach, trying to avoid the patches of light.

I change the tape, put on a long-playing one, and reduce the speed of the tape-recorder from fifteen inches per second to seven and a half. When I listen again I can distinctly hear the motor chugging weaker and stronger. The boat must be making its way through the small mangrove bushes just outside the protected area.

Now there is no longer any doubt. It must be the poachers. I switch on the recorder since the sound of the motor may be perhaps a clue to identification later. Lights start to show and the sound in the earphones gets louder. Beams of light from electric lamps slide over the trees, flashing on the white wings of restless herons. The birds call anxiously, completely trapped at their roosts by the darkness of the night. They can see nothing, have nowhere to fly to. Soon there will be a revolting slaughter with no chance of escape for the birds.

The tongues of light play back and forth over the scene, sliding over the birds as the men use the electric lamps to reckon up their prey. The flock of red ibises, like juicy red berries, sit there waiting to be plucked. Suddenly I can bear it no longer. I let out a yell which even deafens my own ears. The tape-recorder is still running and the sound is recorded. Winston puts his hand on my arm and gives me a warning look. I realise that I am behaving like a madman.

The motor goes silent, the poachers are listening. We are right out on the water with the bush and some dead mangrove skeletons behind us. Minutes go by, but we are somehow removed from time, without substance. We are so close to them that the water lapping against the hull of our boat would give us away if it were not for the noise being made by the birds. Their alarm calls drown other sounds and the dense mangrove roots behind us also serve as camouflage. Obviously the men out there think they must have misheard because they start up their motor again. They have drifted out a little and now come closer to the ibises, scanning the flock with their lights. Then the shooting starts.

The alarm calls cease abruptly, the shots echo while there is a beating of wings like the breaking of waves. The birds cannot escape but remain motionless above the trees and then sink down again in the same place. The twigs crackle again as each bird tries to find a place in the death-trap. The hunters chug around and pick up the dead and wounded birds, while the macabre sounds of dying birds are picked up by the microphone and recorded unemotionally on tape.

Although desperately keen to stop the marauders in some way, I know that the responsibility for what might happen to Winston as well as to myself is mine. Furthermore our boat is full of expensive equipment and just at the moment the tape running so peacefully past the recording head is particularly valuable. I record one more shot before switching off. Our documentary evidence could be of significant value and I decide to remove it from the machine and hide it under the thwarts in case of emergency. The hunters disappear slowly between the clumps while the light gradually creeps like tentacles towards the frightened flocks of herons. We push the boat against the current. Winston punts fast and when we are out of sight we start the motor and drive at top speed for home, taking with us our valuable evidence.

Next day I went to the Forest Department in Port of Spain. There I met Mr Murray, the Chief Game Warden, and reported what had happened. He listened to the tape and was obviously worried. He also took note of my report that I had spent a long time in the protected area without any game warden asking what I was doing or checking my permit. The rangers were then called in one after another and made to listen to the sound-recording. They stood there with earphones on while a stern-faced Mr Murray watched in the background. The effect of the shout recorded on tape was so sudden that a couple of them literally jumped in the air.

It was agreed that a strong force divided between three boats should move into the area in the late afternoon. Spaced out at suitable positions they should have every chance of catching the marauders. Mr Murray arranged for six game rangers to meet us that evening at the place from where we usually started our boat.

When we were well out into the swamp I pointed out suitable places for the other boats and asked one of the rangers to accompany me in ours. We then moved into the mangrove bush where we had spent the previous night. We decided not to build ourselves in as we wanted to be able to move out quickly. Everything was now ready and with the natural barrier of mangroves we reckoned that we had every chance of cutting off any possible retreat within the area.

Darkness fell and the moon shone even brighter than on the previous night. We waited on tenterhooks and then at the same time as on the previous night heard the chugging of a motor-boat with the engine running at low revolutions. The boat appeared and a lamp was reflected in the water. Our companion took the gun out of its leather holster and I heard the muffled click as he released the safety catch.

The boat glided nearer to the tree, but there was something different about it. The light pointed down the whole time and the engine sounded less powerful than on the previous evening. I then realised that it was only a fisherman out spear-fishing. The other two boats appeared and closed in. It was a fine show of strength designed to catch a tiger but all that we had trapped was a mouse. The poor fisherman, with no evil designs on the birds, should nevertheless have been outside the protected area and was booked by the dutiful wardens for a night in the lock-up of Port of Spain. The wardens were triumphant but I was disturbed by the thought that the real miscreants would now be warned.

The next evening when I was going out Dr Jocelyn Crane had a serious talk with me. She had heard how I had become involved and while we ate an early dinner at Simla she explained her point of view, which amounted to a veto on my anti-poaching activities. As director of the research station she was responsible for all the people who lived there, and if anything should happen to me, she would of course be in a difficult situation. Miss Crane was not accustomed to having her authority questioned but I explained to her that in this case I could not back down.

The operation was due to be repeated that evening but when we arrived at the agreed place we found only one of the six men had turned up. The others never appeared due to some misunderstanding. We agreed that the one warden should wait at the arm of the river by which the poachers would probably beat a retreat. If the other game-wardens arrived later, they were to man the most strategic points.

When darkness fell we again heard a series of shots from the area bordering on the Sanctuary, a name which now began to seem inappropriate. After a time we heard more sounds of activity, as evidently one of the roosting trees on the outskirts was providing the best hunting ground. We moved out and punted quickly to the place where we had left our armed man. We found however that he had withdrawn from the area, which was now reeking of gunpowder. I could understand him doing this because he was ludicrously ill-equipped to deal with the poachers. A single rifle and a 5-horse-power motor were no match for automatic guns and the powerful engine of a poacher's motor-boat.

I cursed at the inadequacy of our equipment. Then I had an idea. I took out a box of film, tore off two bits of the black sticky adhesive tape round the metal box and made a cross out of them. Then I lashed the microphone just under the gunwale and hid the tape-recorder under the pieces of sacking which usually served as camouflage. My plan quite simply was to go right up to the 'enemy ship' under friendly but false colours. I thought of playing the innocent and pretending to know nothing about the protected area or protection in general. Leaving the tape-recorder switched on, I hoped to call out to them and ask how to buy one of the pretty red birds they had just shot. If I could act the part sufficiently well and if I offered them 25 to 30 dollars, we ought to be able to chat long enough for their voices on the tape to be usable as evidence. Later on, the finding of their boat in the harbour at Port of Spain should be comparatively simple because I planned to stick the black tape, in the shape of a cross, on the side of their boat while the ibis was changing hands.

I must admit that my pulse rate increased considerably as the distance between the two boats decreased. Winston steered a dead straight course, and we soon made out four dark figures ahead. When we were within talking distance we saw four fishing-rods pointing in our direction. Not guilty! I could scarcely believe it. All thought of my prepared harangue vanished. They had suspected that mischief was brewing and I felt decidedly ridiculous. We glided past in silence.

There was nothing we could do. Needless to say, no more shots were heard that night.

Unfortunately there were no further developments that week as far as I was concerned because I was completely *hors de combat*. I was laid low by a stomach complaint that was going the rounds in Arima. Caused by a virus possibly picked up from eating fruit, it resulted in vomiting which went on for three days without stopping except for intervals of about half an hour. My stomach muscles ached as much as if I had been undergoing rigorous physical training.

All this time I was worrying because I did not know what was happening at Caroni. But when I recovered and could get out onto the marsh again, I forgot all about my troubles. Two boats with poachers, guns and ibises had been caught inside the protected area. I was delighted. There was every chance that peace would reign at last over the terrorised ibis population. The birds needed all the quiet they could get. I decided to remove myself from the scene at Caroni and to start occupying myself seriously with what is perhaps the most interesting of Trinidad's birds—the oilbird.

# 4 *Birds in eternal darkness*

I had originally intended to film the oilbirds in Venezuela at the place where they were discovered by Alexander von Humboldt. It was in 1799 that this German scientist entered a cave with a group of Indian guides and first saw these strange birds. Von Humboldt named them *Steatornis caripensis*, *Steatornis* meaning simply oilbird, and *caripensis* referring to the place, Caripe, where the cave is situated. The Indians were convinced that the spirits of the dead dwelt in the interior of the cave. They did not dare go into the farther recesses, for to do so meant joining one's deceased relatives and hence dying. This superstition has probably helped save the oilbird as a species. It has no other form of protection from man, which perhaps is just as well since in most places man carries out his guard duties as effectively as a fox set to keep watch over geese.

At that time the Indians made use of the oilbirds to supply oil for food and fuel. The young birds are exceedingly plump and the Indians knocked them down from ledges in the caves where they sat in rows, and then roasted their harvest over fires. The oil thus obtained could be used for lighting flares, enabling the Indians to penetrate a little farther in from the mouth of the cave and kill yet more young.

The oilbird is a strange creature, completely adapted for an existence that is often in total darkness. The greatest illumination it ever experiences is the white light of a full moon, shining down out of the velvet-black tropical night. This gives the birds more than enough light to find the palms and other trees where they forage.

The oilbirds are in fact vegetarian. In this they differ from their closest relatives, the owls and nightjars, which live on animal food. Other details concerning their relationship are rather difficult to determine, but analyses of egg-white proteins (Sibley, 1960) suggest that their closest relatives are the nightjars. The oilbird is, however, placed systematically in its own species and genus, and in its own family, the Steatornithidae.

This large bird, which measures almost three feet between the wing tips, has many remarkable characteristics. It has an excellent sense of smell, which is unusual in birds in general but probably necessary to enable them to find fruits of the right kind and ripeness. Their sight is presumably good but no research has been done on it. On the other hand investigations indicate without doubt that the birds can manœuvre in their caves in the absence of any light at all.

*Guacharo*, as the oilbird is called in Venezuela, means roughly 'he who shrieks and groans.' It was this shrieking from the depths of the Caripe cave which frightened the Indians and kept them from going right in. By contrast it inspired the American zoologist Donald R. Griffin to penetrate so far that all the light from the mouth of the cave was excluded.

Following a long series of investigations Dr Griffin has thrown fresh light on the orientation mechanisms of bats, and the results of these investigations are now largely familiar even to those who are only moderately interested in natural history. Everyone knows that bats orientate in pitch-dark with the help of echo-location. They emit short series of squeaks which are of such high frequency that the human ear cannot perceive them.

Von Humboldt's description of the incredible din caused by the loud calls of hundreds of birds in the interior of the cave made Dr Griffin suspect that echo-location might be used by them when flying in the dark; his theory was confirmed as a result of a series of experiments. In the deepest parts of the cave, where the birds made clicking sounds as they flew around, he pointed a camera in the direction of the cave entrance and exposed the film by leaving the shutter open. After half an hour of this, he developed the film. It revealed not the slightest trace of the presence of light. So far it was quite clear that the birds were able to orientate without the slightest help from light.

By releasing captured birds in an experimental enclosure he established that they avoided walls and other obstacles in pitch-dark with apparent ease, but as soon as their ears were stopped up they bumped into things.

Griffin also recorded the sounds made by the birds and with the help of these he was able to establish that the clicking orientation noises lasted one or two thousandths of a second—a frequency of about 7,000 per second: a sound completely audible to the human ear, which under good conditions can perceive sound frequencies up to 20,000, but which does not react to the sound emitted by bats at approximately 100,000 per second.

The cave at Caripe is always occupied by hundreds of *guacharos*

ABOVE *A day's march through the difficult country of the rain-forest up to the oilbird caves on Mount Aripo is both tiring and thirsty work. A piece cut off a so-called water vine gives Elliot a full glass of refreshing water which is filtered by the plant itself and makes an excellent drink.* BELOW *The entrance lies so well hidden in the luxuriant vegetation that we could smell the cave long before we saw it.*

OVERLEAF LEFT *Admiring the roof of the cave which has a drapery of stalactites: John Dunston, Elliot Olton, and the author. The oilbirds live two floors farther down.* OVERLEAF RIGHT *While incubating, the oilbird sits in a shallow saucer-like nest formed from regurgitated material and excrement. Regurgitated kernels of palms and other plants germinate alongside the nest, producing yellowish-white shoots.*

CENTRE SPREAD *The oilbird has a wing-span of 3 feet and when flying in the caves has a dancing, fluttering flight. The wing surface, about 220 square inches, is very large for a bird weighing rather under a pound; it enables the oilbird to carry masses of food in the crop during the flights from the feeding places, which are often many miles from the caves.*

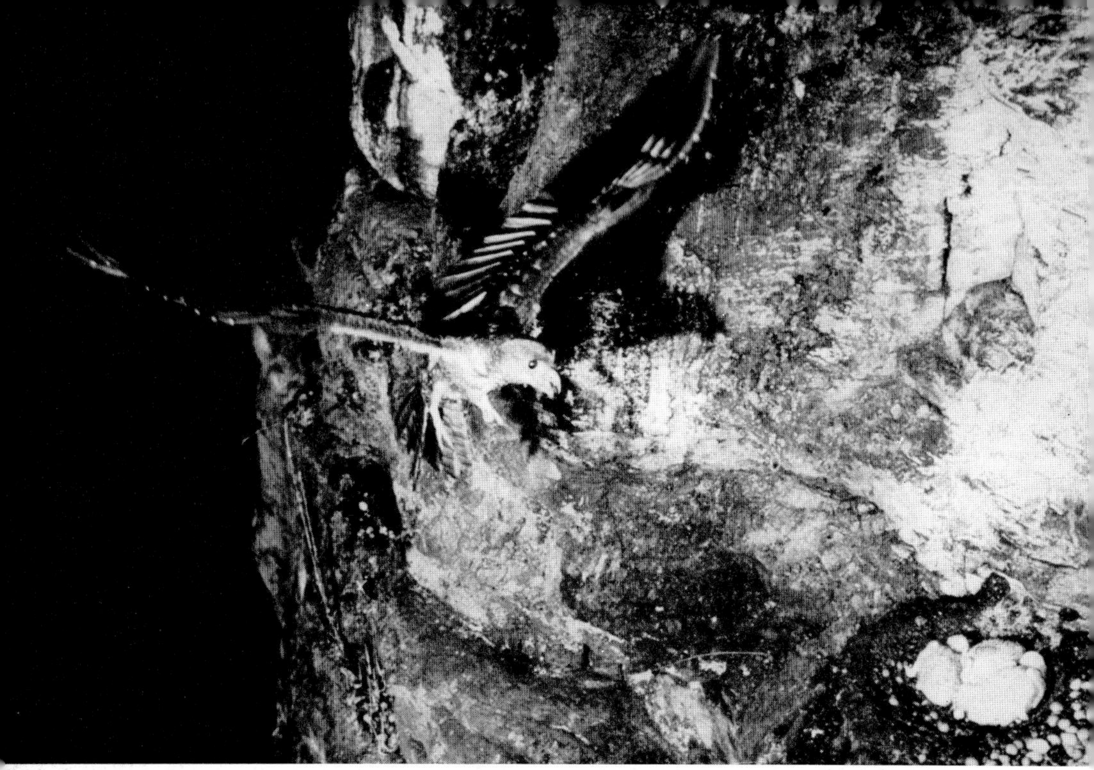

and has become a considerable tourist attraction. In order to humour the tourists, lighting of various colours has been installed. This may sound slightly nauseating but from my point of view it had the advantage that electric current would be available for the lamps essential for the filming.

Instead of Caripe I used four other caves in Trinidad as my 'hunting' grounds. Even on this island, which, like Venezuela, is overflowing with oil—or more precisely with petroleum—it is ironical that the oilbirds should have been utilised for their combined value as food and fuel. So far there are thirteen known caves where oilbirds are to be found and of these five have been worked out. The remaining eight are so inaccessible that they have remained virtually untouched.

There is one cave which is relatively approachable. I have reason to be grateful for this because one of my top priorities was the filming of the birds in the dark, using infra-red, invisible light. Without this

ABOVE *When the young are as large as this they have already developed the powerful hooked beak with which they will soon be able to pluck fruits from the trees. To avoid being injured the parent turns to face the edge of the nest. The young nibbles the adult in the region of the tail . . .* BELOW *. . . and the adult quickly turns round and pushes its beak into the hungry gape. This method of feeding the young is a very good example of adaptation to an environment where sight cannot help the birds to aim accurately. Note the ring on the leg; this bird was ringed at the same nest by David Snow seven years before this picture was taken.*

PREVIOUS TWO PAGES, ABOVE LEFT *The oilbird hovers in front of its nest with its beak open while emitting a series of clicking sounds. This system of echo-location does not seem to be particularly efficient as the bird may make repeated attempts before finding the correct 'pattern of echoes' for a successful landing.* BELOW LEFT *In certain passages in this cave, where the Oropuche river floods, so little space is left between the rock ceiling and the rushing water that we could scarcely get through them with our equipment.*

RIGHT *The oilbird has developed enormous vocal powers which drown the noise of rivers with their waterfalls in the cave. The long bristles in the area of the beak function as tactile organs in the pitch-darkness.*

particular cave it would have been almost impossible to achieve. Known as Diablotin Cave, although not a cave in the strict sense, it consists of a series of large chambers between a confused mass of gigantic cliffs. There is a river or stream, the Guacharo River, running through the system of chambers, which combines with other streams to form the River Arima. The word *arima* denotes water in the old Carib tongue.

Diablotin Cave, the Devil's Cave, is situated in a large cocoa plantation which belongs to Mrs Asa Wright. Her guests consist partly of those who simply wish to refresh themselves in pleasant tropical surroundings, and partly of zoologists, botanists and others who have some special work to do in the area. Mrs Wright's bungalow is particularly suitable for such guests, being surrounded by nature in abundance.

The oilbird is, of course, the prize exhibit and the cave is visited at least once a week. The birds are accustomed to human disturbance and readily give a demonstration of the screaming for which they are renowned. In spite of the fact that their range of distribution includes mountain districts in Peru, Ecuador, Colombia, Panama, Venezuela, Guyana and northern Brazil, I believe it is true to say that all the pictures in reference books and in other publications originate from this cave.

At Spring Hill, as Asa Wright's plantation is called, I met John Dunston for the first time. He is an engineer at a textile factory in Arima and very interested in natural history. Now and then he drives up to Spring Hill and often guides the guests to Diablotin Cave. We became good friends and he also accompanied me on visits to the other caves.

John Dunston has had a great deal of experience with oilbirds. During the years when the British biologist David Snow made his extensive investigations into the food and breeding biology of the oilbird, John was his constant companion and at that time they visited most of the caves. Without John's help it would have been practically impossible for me to find the caves because they lie in a confusing terrain of rain-forest in which the hills and valleys all look alike.

John happened to come over to Simla while I was suffering from the stomach trouble which I mentioned in the last chapter. When he knew I was worried that I might pass on the infection to the others at the research station, he suggested I should go back with him to Arima as the people in his area had all suffered from a bout of the same kind of sickness. This solved my problems as Caroni was also easier to reach from Arima than from Simla. In addition I would have the benefit of John's valuable help in filming the oilbird cave in Oropuche, which was by no means as accessible as Diablotin Cave.

The oilbirds often choose a cave with running water, hot and cold I was about to say, but the comforts in Oropuche were not quite up to this standard. The River Oropuche runs far up into the long winding cave, an imposing phenomenon with low passages and high vaults covered with stalactites. The route into the cave is exacting, especially if one is carrying expensive and sensitive apparatus. The bed of the surprisingly chilly stream is a confusion of sharp blocks and unpredictable holes. Through John's efforts I was offered the assistance of a group of men from the factory where he worked, who were keen to see the cave and help with the filming. Among other things we were equipped with three powerful, battery-driven searchlights, which were to illuminate the vaults which hitherto had never been exposed to the light. Before we visited the cave we had to sign a piece of paper showing that the owner of the land disclaimed any responsibility for what might happen there. The reason for this was a tragic incident the year before in which two young men were drowned.

There is no doubt that the cave conveys an impression of foreboding and the narrow passages are distinctly trying for people with a tendency to claustrophobia. One of my friends was in fact forced to give up. In one of the passages we had to wade for a long stretch crouching under a low rock ceiling, which forced us to keep so close to the water surface that the film camera and other equipment narrowly escaped getting wet.

The battery-driven Sun-guns that we planned to use are capable of running for twenty minutes, giving a light of 350 watts. The effective time for filming is quite short, bearing in mind the preparatory work which involves installing the lights, setting up the camera, taking light readings, and so on. We therefore made four trips to Oropuche in all. The last one took place at the height of the rainy season. The rains had stopped a couple of days before, but in spite of this the water level in some of the passages was so high that we had to be extremely careful in getting the equipment along the low tunnels.

Luck was really with us on this occasion. On the way home from the cave we were half-drowned by a powerful and lengthy downpour. If we had been caught in the cave beyond the approach tunnel, the flood would have closed the passage and we would have been forced either to stay inside or to travel underwater for about twenty yards.

In addition to the oilbirds there are a number of other light-shy organisms to be seen in the passages. One has to watch where to put one's hands, for certain surfaces are occupied by many specimens of a kind of scorpion which looks like a very large spider. These probably live on the animals that feed on the faeces of the birds and bats.

A whole chapter could be written about the bats alone. Trinidad has fifty-eight species, which provide Dr Griffin and his colleagues with a very large field for investigation. Amongst other things the ability of the bats to orientate over long distances is being investigated

*The visual purple pigment shines like a 'stop' traffic light in the oilbird's light-sensitive eye. The bird has a well-developed sense of smell and good hearing but —most remarkable of all—like a bat it can orientate in total darkness by means of echo-location.*

and work on this was still going on when I travelled home. A young research couple, Jane and Tim Williams, collected bats in certain caves and released them late in the evening. Each experimental animal was equipped with a tiny lamp so that the direction it took could be observed. However, even with field-glasses difficulty was experienced in keeping track of the routes taken by the small 'lanterns' and the two research workers were gradually changing their methods and going over to the use of a tiny radio transmitter, which was fastened on to the bats. This may sound a heavy burden for so small a creature but it is of course normal for a bat to carry its two young in flight.

One of the caves occupied by these animals has a low entrance which is piled high with loose slabs of slate. These require careful negotiation or they start to collapse. Inside the vaulted chamber, the floor is as soft as a close-fitting carpet. It is made up of a crawling mass of living organisms, small brownish animals, long white thread-like objects and, perhaps most splendid of all, some shiny yellowish-brown cockroaches two inches long. The cockroaches are dotted all over the surface of the floor when you enter the chamber but disappear at high speed. In a couple of seconds they dig themselves down under the mass of small animals and the surface then heaves slowly, looking like a snuff-coloured sea in a gentle swell.

All these animals live on the manna that falls every day, the excreta of the bats. Two species of bat are present in this chamber, *Phyllostomus hastatus*, a large species, and *Carollia perspicillata*, which is smaller. Both of these are fruit-eating species, and this is probably why the floor-covering provides the right conditions, from

*When we turned on our lights in the cave, it was possibly the first time in hundreds of thousands of years that this species had seen any light stronger than that of the full moon. The collective sound from the screams of over two hundred frightened birds was decidedly painful to our eardrums.*

the point of view of nutrition and consistency, for the animal population that skulks in the deposits of excreta. As you go into the cave you are also aware of a remarkable odour, which cannot be described as an aroma likely to attract the tourist.

When you turn on a searchlight and shine it among the resting animals, everything springs into life and there is an indescribable confusion of thousands of wings. Something else remarkable happens: the temperature in the cave rises sharply as a result of the physical exertions of the animals, which increase their body temperature. It is a completely involuntary method of heating the chamber and the warm atmosphere gradually becomes nauseating. All the exhaled humidity of the small animals is mixed with something which looks like fine rain in the beam of light; it is, in fact, a spray of urine from the frightened creatures. This gradually abates and finally stops. One's clothes become so sour from the spray that it is advisable to throw them away after a visit to the caves.

Although only a rustle of fluttering wings can be heard, the chamber is in actual fact filled by a giant chorus of powerful shrieks—but, at a frequency of up to 100,000 per second, these are inaudible to the human ear. In spite of the fact that the bats ought to be able to avoid people they bump against you frequently; they climb about on your clothes or on the back of your head or over your face. When they flutter against you before flitting away, their wings are surprisingly cold as they touch you.

The author of a claustrophobic horror story would have plenty of realistic background material if he set the scene in such a cave. It is not difficult to imagine what would happen if the pile of loose slabs collapsed and blocked the exit. The plot could develop along various lines but eventually the trapped person would be forced through sheer fatigue to take a rest on the floor amongst the heap of crawling animals. Hungry cockroaches might swarm over his body; exhausted but still game, the victim would doubtless stagger to his feet again and totter around in the darkness, while the atmosphere became more and more deficient in oxygen; finally, overcome with exhaustion, the character would lose consciousness as he collapsed on to the soft heap of writhing animals. One other horrific detail could be added: the fear of disease.

The small flying mammals are often infected with tuberculosis, and just to breathe the air in the caves brings a risk of infection, not to mention the danger of catching rabies, which is particularly liable to be transmitted by the bite of the two species of vampire bat. Other species of bat beside the vampires can also be infected. Biologists doing research work are not allowed to start work in the caves until they have had injections against rabies.

Much more could be said about bats but my primary objective in visiting the caves was to film the oilbirds. I was anxious to observe them under undisturbed conditions and to record the calls they made before they were alarmed by the paraphernalia of filming. When we left the bats we therefore turned off the lights and covered the rest of the distance in the dark. We stumbled along the last stretch of the stream under cover of darkness, placing our feet at strange angles among the rocks, whose sharp edges projected without any consideration for our safety.

As we made our way to the main chamber a bird flew backwards and forwards in front of us. In the pitch-dark the reverberating sounds gave a good demonstration of the principles of echo-location. The short echoes became longer and one could tell by ear when the cave was widening. Birds flew at us like spirits of the dark, rattling and whirring as they alternately approached and withdrew.

The sound made by the wings, which are the size of a buzzard's, was distinctly audible. Short squeaks could also be heard among the beating of wings, evidently made by the young which were up on the ledges. The only other sound was the rippling of water.

We knew when we had reached the main chamber by the lengthening of the echoes caused by the shrieks of the birds. It was obvious that the auditorium was pretty large and I decided to set up the filming equipment there. We delayed turning on the light until the last minute so as to film the whole mass of birds together. We also wanted to count their number as far as this was possible. Switching on the light would inevitably create a gigantic disturbance. The light from our three Sun-guns would in effect bring the equivalent of daylight to a cave which had remained in total darkness for hundreds of thousands, perhaps millions, of years. It would be the first time that the birds had ever experienced any light stronger than that of a full moon. However, having seen the birds in Diablotin Cave at Spring Hill quietly return to their ledges after similar shock treatment, I had the feeling that the adults here would soon do the same.

At last everything was ready. I started to run the film camera and shouted: 'Lights on!' In a flash the cave was bathed in light. Hundreds of red eyes were directed towards us and seconds after it seemed as though my eardrums would burst. It was like being attacked by thousands of Red Indians, although even this is an inadequate description. The big birds fluttered around like lightweight butterflies, screaming raucously. After some seconds I shouted: 'Lights off!'

Once again the cave was in pitch-darkness. The screams were cut off as abruptly as if a sound tape had broken but instead a barrage of clicks echoed through the large chamber. It was as though we were in a gigantic watchmaker's shop. With the change from light to darkness, all the birds circling overhead had immediately switched over to their automatic pilot.

We turned the light on and off again a couple of times with the same result—shrieks in the light, clicks in the dark. We then kept the lights on and the fluttering mob gradually seemed to quieten down and the screams became much fewer. After only a few minutes the birds all returned to the ledges and shuffled nervously around their homes on their small, peculiarly positioned feet. Their bodies leant forwards at an angle, as though slung in a cradle; their tails were raised in the air and their bills were hooked, like those of birds of prey, making them appear almost aggressive. Their large eyes gazed down on us like red flashlights, while their heads moved from side to side in owl-like fashion.

Occasionally something rattled on the cliff wall. It was the kernels of fruit being knocked down by the birds as they moved around. Below the ledges there were piles of debris, a yard high and variegated in colour. The droppings were mixed in with everything else, including a flora of toadstools. Thin, pale stems, four or five inches long, stuck up out of the heaps like nails on a fakir's board; these were palms and other plants, which would never develop any further.

I walked a few yards back so as to get the whole scene into perspective, trying to get the people manning the lights and the oilbirds into the same frame. From this position I had a remarkable picture. The whole company seemed to be standing in the jaws of a gigantic dragon. The stalactites hanging from the roof became the giant teeth in the upper jaw of the dragon; the lower jaw was made up of stalagmites, corresponding calcareous deposits which stood six feet high. The oilbirds turned into hobgoblins, milling around inside the giant gape of this king of the mountain, passing in and out of the gaps between the monster's teeth. If von Humboldt's Indian companions had witnessed the same sight their superstitions would certainly have been confirmed.

Looking like a giant toothpick, there was a long pole resting against the giant's snout. There were steps carved up this primitive step-ladder. It was difficult to determine its age but judging by its appearance it looked as though it had been made not so long ago and used fairly recently for harvesting oil. We estimated that there were about two hundred birds in the cave and plenty of young were also present.

As we came away from the cave for the last time we were met by a man who asked us if we had been out hunting. I started to explain that we had been into the cave but then I decided it would be wise to imply that all was not well inside. I replied quite truthfully that I would never go back into the cave—I had already paid four visits to it—and, pretending to be in a state of shock, I reminded him that two people had been drowned there and that only one body had been recovered. As to the other . . .

The man slowly widened his eyes and gaped at me; he explained that he too knew that the cave was haunted and that we had been lucky to get out again. He was, of course, completely convinced that if one of the scientists from Simla had seen supernatural things in the cave, then the place was definitely taboo. Perhaps that unfortunate drowning may, after all, have served a useful purpose: superstition can be an effective deterrent, and the oilbird's foot-hold in the cave could well benefit from such protection.

# 5 *Seeing in the dark*

The visits to Oropuche yielded the first film sequences of oilbirds ever to be taken, but of course the film showed the birds in a completely unnatural situation as the pictures were taken when the birds were subjected to a much stronger light than anything they had previously experienced. Whenever possible I like to film animals under natural, undisturbed conditions. This could not be done in the caves but I hoped to add something to our knowledge of these creatures, known as diablotins or devil birds, which live in the Diablotin Cave.

Many scientists have taken an interest in the oilbirds since the days of von Humboldt. I have already mentioned Donald Griffin's series of investigations which showed that the clicking sounds made by the *guacharos* are pulses by which they echo-locate. The scientist who has made the most intensive study of this species so far is David Snow. He made a detailed investigation into their habits over a period of three and a half years. Amongst other things he studied the distribution of oilbirds in Trinidad, the number of birds present in the thirteen breeding localities, and details of their breeding biology, including the number of eggs, the development and diet of the young, and so on. His two papers in *Zoologica* provide a wealth of data assembled with such care and skill that one might wonder what still remains to be found out about this species. Everything about oilbirds appears to be already known except for one aspect of their behaviour which might turn out to be the most important of all: how do they behave in total darkness? How do oilbirds manœuvre, how well can their ears 'see,' and what is the nocturnal behaviour of the parents vis-à-vis the young?

Darkness is a relative term. The blackest night at our darkest time of year is not really dark providing that one has the visual acuity of a tawny owl. I carried out some research at Stockholm University over three years on the visual cells of owls. In a series of tests on five species, I found that the tawny owl has a retina that is more sensitive to light than that of any other species or, to be more precise, it has the lowest threshold value to light. A light with a strength of 0.00000016 foot-candle is sufficient for a tawny owl's eyes to be able to discern a grey mouse on white sand at a distance of just over two yards. The tests were made with the light from a candle shining on to the prey from a distance of about five hundred yards, the candle being placed behind it.

In the interior of the cave where the oilbirds live, even a tawny owl would not be able to see, nor I without the help of a special piece of equipment, which is called an image intensifier or sniperscope. Without this artificial aid I would have been unable to see anything. The sniperscope consists of a searchlight in which the visible light is filtered off, leaving behind the invisible infra-red light which is directed towards the object. Field-glasses fitted with a small slide receive the reflected infra-red light and when pointed at an object the picture is transformed into a visible greenish image. In the Second World War the sniperscope was used during night fighting. I found it very valuable, for instance, during my observations on owls both in the laboratories of the Zoological Institution in Stockholm and out in the field.

ABOVE *The coral-snake,* Micrurus circinalis, *is so small that it would fit into the palm of your hand, but it would scarcely be wise to place it there. Like all the other coral-snakes it is very venomous.* BELOW *I searched for the extremely rare bushmaster both day and night all the time I was in Trinidad but I never succeeded in finding one. This specimen from Brazil was about 6 feet long, but the species has been known to reach a length of 11 feet.*

These 'magic' glasses were particularly suitable for use in the oil-bird caves and I was able to see the birds in a pale green light without disturbing them. The pictures of birds flying, landing, feeding their young and so on, were all taken with the aid of the sniperscope, using it as a viewfinder. It would have been completely impossible to get the pictures otherwise, because one must be able to choose the precise moment for setting off the electronic flash. The sniperscope thus opens up new opportunities for fascinating glimpses into another world.

Before leaving home on my travels, I got in touch with one of the experts in the Swedish Defence Research Department, for I wanted to learn about the possible application of infra-red techniques to filming. The use of infra-red presents certain difficulties but I was fortunate in that the expert whom I consulted, Sverre Calmbrant, took my problems as seriously as though they were part of his own work. We made a series of measurements in a darkroom with infra-red film of various kinds, taking pictures of a stuffed eagle owl, using different filters, different light sources and varying distances in order to get some norms as a basis from which to work. I was much impressed by the way in which Sverre Calmbrant became absorbed in a subject so remote to him.

It was not until I was in Trinidad that I learnt from a Swedish newspaper article that Sverre Calmbrant was the man who was responsible for a masterly piece of detection. Working with only a short strip of unexposed film he discovered after a number of experiments the special process required to develop the film used by the 'spy colonel' Wennerstrom. Once the method was exposed, the colonel's confession soon followed.

ABOVE *The fer-de-lance is a menace in large areas of South America; it is easily irritated and has a very fast-acting venom.* BELOW *The graceful movements of a snake never cease to fascinate me. It was wonderful to see an anaconda, especially in its right element—water.*

It was from Sverre Calmbrant that I learnt of the existence of a new, very sensitive 16mm infra-red film. I telephoned an order for some to New York in advance. The sensitivity of infra-red film to invisible infra-red heat waves is enormous compared with that of other film. Bearing in mind that I would be using it under tropical conditions this sensitivity to heat was certain to be crucial. The problems of handling the film under such conditions were roughly equivalent to moving along a tightrope wearing a pair of skates.

I collected the infra-red stock in New York on a cold day in January and packed it immediately into a refrigerated box. Trinidad's lovely climate of 30° Centigrade (86°F) is lethal to infra-red film. If the box had been left in Piarco's hot warehouse during the three days it took me to clear my equipment through the Customs, the film would have turned completely black and no nocturnal filming of the oilbirds would have been possible. Fortunately I was able to get at the particular package in time and it was safely in the deep freeze at Simla before the blocks of ice surrounding the stock had melted. Disaster had only narrowly been avoided.

The film was removed from the deep-freeze and thawed out in the refrigerator before each night of filming. It was transported to the filming location in a refrigerated box and then transferred into a chilled pocket in the rucksack to be taken out finally in the cool night temperature of the cave. After each night of filming it was taken in a refrigerated box to Port of Spain, where the heat of the sun practically melted the asphalt on the roads. The refrigerated box was then sent to an air-conditioned laboratory, which was always warned in advance so that there were people ready to develop the film without delay.

I had proof of the extreme sensitivity of the film one day when I accidentally allowed a roll of film to fall out of the chilled pocket at the top of the rucksack. I was making my way home and the roll must have slipped down against the warmth of my back. The whole length of the roll went coal-black for half its width.

There are many problems attached to filming with infra-red stock.

Every time a new subject is taken, it is necessary to do a test. Infra-red light varies in the way it is reflected according to the nature of the surface of the object, and there are no exposure tables or light meters available from which to take readings. Test exposures are therefore the only answer. A further problem arises when the focus is set in normal light, which was the only possible method for me to use. After setting for normal light, the distance value must then be adjusted and the setting altered from, for example, 3 metres to 2.7 metres. This is because infra-red light has a different refractive index from visible light.

I realised that filming the oilbirds in Oropuche Cave would be an extremely difficult operation. The problem of transporting the equipment was a major headache in itself. Car batteries, sniperscope, filter-holders, three camera tripods, searchlights with batteries, film camera with batteries, equipment for still photography and electronic flash all had to be taken out every morning and dried because of the humidity. The equipment also had to be cleaned every time after use, due to the bird and bat droppings. Then all of it had to be lugged into the cave the following evening.

Mrs Wright made fun of us when she saw us setting off on our expeditions, laden like donkeys. She had willingly given me permission to film in her cave, which she guards with loving care, and, of course, she had also allowed Dr Snow to use the same place for his investigations. We had to build a platform inside the cave from which to film the oilbirds. John Dunston helped me with this, together with one of Mrs Wright's men who answered to the name of Fatty. He was of sturdy build and always laughing; no Swedish labourer would have approved of this form of address. Good-natured tolerance appears to be the chief virtue of the people of Trinidad. Fatty lived up to his name magnificently and carried two gigantic beams of wood to the cave without apparent trouble.

We lowered the beams down to the mouth of the cave and then set about sawing them up, ready for constructing the platform inside the cave. We made so much noise that I feared the birds would be disturbed. As we heaved the planks into position in the cave and wedged them in cavities and against corners, every sound was amplified. We built the platform on a site facing all the nests and when it was finished we retired to a discreet distance. We were most relieved to see that the birds quickly flew back to the nests, as though nothing had happened. It is worth mentioning that in spite of my regular visits to the site which took place over a period of a month, the oilbirds in this cave had their best breeding season. In the nests in front of the platform, 25 young developed to full maturity.

I often waited until all the adult birds had flown out before moving into position inside the cave. This involved carrying the heavy equipment through the rushing water, over a long, flat step-bridge, and up on to the platform as quickly as possible. I would then set up the equipment, switch on the searchlight with its powerful visible light, make all the adjustments, turn the light out again and then sit still and absolutely silent throughout the night. It was 3.30am when the birds left the cave on their last feeding trip. They never took any notice of me.

One of the factors that contributed to the good breeding results was that almost every night I was able to remove one or two large mountain crabs from the immediate vicinity of the nests. These strong crabs nip the young birds repeatedly, eating them alive while the area of the wounds grows. I watched this happening one night in the sniperscope at a ledge out of my reach. After this I was unable to resist the temptation to interfere with something which strictly speaking is nature's business, for I do not usually tamper with the natural course of events. The crabs in Oropuche are also a serious menace to the adult *guacharos*. Now and again we found crabs right at the end of the winding paths of the caves, just where the stream

*In the dark vistas of the rain-forest the motmot, a bird the size of a jay, can be heard giving its stifled call, from which its name is derived. In most of the eight species the two longest tail-feathers end in small racquet tips.*

flowed up from below. One of these crabs had a whole batch of eggs and young under its tail.

The nocturnal trips to Diablotin Cave were not without excitement. John would call out a warning to beware of snakes. When working as a road engineer he had seen men from his work-gang struck in the neck by bushmasters and fer-de-lance, while working on the slopes. I swept my miner's lamp from side to side all the time I was trying to brace my feet in the slippery mud, stumbling over the large tree-roots and up and down the muddy slopes through the small water-courses. I let out an oath every so often when the heavy photographic equipment slipped and threw me off balance. Unfortunately I never got a glimpse of a bushmaster or fer-de-lance, or of one of the two handsome species of coral-snake, during any of these nocturnal promenades.

The nights spent on the platform were among the most interesting and fascinating of any that I have experienced. To the naked eye there is nothing but total darkness. With the sniperscope a door opens on to a completely new and secret world, in which the shimmer of green in the scope adds to the sensation of unreality. The cave comes to life at 7 o'clock, one hour after sunset, when the true darkness descends. There is a new peak of activity which replaces the monotony of a day spent meditating in the oilbird colony. The thin necks of the young birds sway like pale plant stalks in a cellar; their eyes are closed, but their beaks grope about and nibble at the parents in the pitch dark. The birds cannot see anything but I can observe their movements through the sniperscope. The chorus of hungry voices rises and falls, making a sound picture which is in complete

ABOVE *The prehensile-tailed porcupine is a rodent with nocturnal habits. The prehensile tail grips with its upper side. Another characteristic feature of the animal is the peculiar clown-like nose, an organ with large air-filled spaces.*
BELOW *The two-toed anteater is very rare. In spite of its popular name it always avoids the poisonous ants. Precisely what it eats during its nocturnal wanderings has yet to be discovered.*

contrast to the comparative quiet of the cave by day. Now and then a bird rattles out from the ledges; then more and more take to the air, joining up into groups which navigate in the dark with their echolocating clicks.

They leave the cave in groups, flying off to a plantation of palms a few miles away. They fly fast over long distances but in the cave, in spite of their wide wing-span, flutter lightly around with ethereal grace. The cave empties and for about two hours there is only the monotonous sound of water as I sit waiting for the birds to return. The young are silent, their round bodies bloated with fat and lying like sacks, moving rhythmically as they breathe. Once the adults have flown out there is no further sound from the young.

The long wait gave me plenty of time to speculate on why the young birds should be so corpulent. Dr Snow weighed young birds of different ages with great care. They develop very slowly and remain in the nest for approximately four months. Indeed, one young bird stayed a total of 168 days, much longer than any bird of the same size range. The newly hatched chicks weigh 12-15 grams; this increases to a maximum of about 625 grams when the young are 70-80 days old. The parents weigh at least 400 grams and the young gradually lose weight from approximately the seventieth day of life till they are ready to fly after 40-50 days of fasting.

Snow has developed his views on this subject in one of his papers. He considers that the transition from a (supposed) insect diet to a vegetarian diet is the explanation for the young putting on fat. Vegetarian food is poor in protein and therefore there is a corresponding lengthening of the period of development. I do not believe, however, that this is the whole story nor even the most important part of it. Fruit-eating birds of the same size, for example parrots and toucans, which live in the same area and are as gregarious as oilbirds, do not have a particularly long period in the nest. It is true that the protein content of their food is higher than that of the oilbird, but since the oilbird chick has already reached the adult's weight by its 45th to 50th day, Snow's reasoning scarcely meets the point.

My theory is that the long period of development is correlated with the complicated nervous system of the oilbird. Compared with the bats the oilbirds are gigantic flying machines. In spite of a 3-foot wing-span they are capable of manœuvring along complicated passages. The ability to judge the distance of its own body from other objects in the dark must require an extensive nervous system which is almost unique among birds. The cave swiftlets, which make the nests used by the Chinese for bird's-nest soup, are also able to echo-locate but they do not seek out their cave until evening. The oilbirds feed in darkness and live and die without ever seeing the light of day. The cerebellum, the nerve centre for balance, is consequently unusually large in them. There is no doubt that their sight is excellent and their sense of smell well developed, which is rare in birds.

Without exaggeration one can say that this highly developed nervous system puts the oilbird in a special class; its brain is certainly the most complicated one in the bird world. Parallel organisms in the animal kingdom with highly developed nervous systems, as for example men, need a long time for development from the embryo to the fully grown adult. The oilbird cannot afford to make a single mistake when it tries to navigate. The surroundings are dangerous—one misjudgement and the young would be carried to certain death by the water. I am convinced that these are the factors which determine the length of the period spent by the young in the nest.

To develop this theory still further, the nesting ledges are often damp and after a heavy downpour has increased the water streaming through the caves there may well be heavy condensation, with masses of water running down the walls. In parts of the distribution range of the oilbird the night temperatures may be dangerously cool. A thick layer of down would be totally inadequate, indeed quite unsuitable for the retention of heat. The fatty tissue of the young oilbird is the answer to the problem of insulation. Marine mammals and birds, for example penguins, have also developed this type of insulating material.

After a long wait in the cave, during which my speculations have had free rein, a clicking sound comes nearer and announces the return of the first oilbird, which is visible through the sniperscope. It dives into the beams of 'invisible' light like a dancing butterfly. Out in the centre of the cave the clicking sounds are very few per unit of time, but as the bird approaches its nest the rate increases until it sounds roughly like the clatter of an accelerating sewing-machine.

When the bird is only a yard from the nest, it casts around again, moving out towards the centre of the cave. It flounders about with its body erect and flapping its wings. Then one hears a new series of accelerating pulses; once again it goes practically up to the nest, only to move out again. This manœuvring is repeated a number of times until perhaps at the seventh or eighth approach the outstretched feet touch the ledge, and the series of clicks ceases abruptly. The young are silent while the female sits on the edge of the nest; when she touches a chick, it screeches and fences with her beak, its long neck fully stretched and its eyes closed.

The chick is quite small, perhaps 25 days old, and the begging call is still quite squeaky. The young one begs obstinately for food for a long time, and the two siblings also start to sway with their worm-like necks. The female lowers her bill until it reaches into the gape of the young chick and then, with pumping movements which go on for half a minute, she fills up the gulping funnel. She feeds each chick in the same way.

More birds start to arrive, each one landing after the same unsure navigation. It is evident that the 7,000 pulses per second emitted by the birds draw an 'echo contour' which is considerably more blurred than that of the bats, which produce short-wave sound pulses.

In the nests which have older chicks, the adult birds get a much rougher reception. I watched one with three large chicks that were about a hundred days old; they were in adult plumage but were still not fledged. I saw a parent bird land—whether it was male or female I could not tell, as the sexes are identical. I then witnessed a type of behaviour which is unique to the oilbird and for which it appears to be well adapted.

The parent bird simply turns its back towards the young, who repeatedly nip the adult in the back, making fast darting movements with their beaks. This appears to stimulate the regurgitation of food. It is possible to see food coming up and at the right moment the adult turns round and releases the food into the gape of the chick that made the nip. The adult turns its back again, and waits with its stern facing the chicks until the next portion of food arrives in its beak. This behaviour is unquestionably practical: to have three powerful beaks in the face can be dangerous. With its beak an oilbird can easily pluck off a palm fruit, and a palm fruit is very firmly attached.

While the young are being fed they constantly call out like squeaky hinges. When the adults have finished feeding the chicks they fly off, clicking like a lot of telegraph lines, and the young lapse into immediate silence. The adults assemble as previously into small groups which fly out into the night light again. Compared with the darkness in the cave the black, starlit sky is very bright. I noticed that on every occasion I accompanied the birds out of the cave, the clicking always stopped just as they emerged into the night sky. The birds had no need to echo-locate as their eyesight in normal darkness is uncommonly good.

The only person who had heard the birds clicking outside the cave is John Dunston. One night when he was driving on the Blanchisseuse mountain road and along the valley, he heard a peculiar rattling sound. He thought that something had caught in the wheel and stopped. He then heard quite clearly the rapping sound of a group of oilbirds. The explanation must have been that the car lights struck the birds as he drove over the brow of a hill and blinded them, thus releasing the echo-location mechanism.

At the end of a long vigil in the cave I faced the wearisome task of gathering the equipment together. When all was quiet again in the cave I stretched my cramped limbs and then packed all the filming gear together, ready for carrying it out along the tortuous passages where I splashed my way through torrents of water. The equipment always seemed much heavier on the return journey.

People who have never done any bird-watching always imagine it to be a very tedious business. In fact I was never bored during my nights in the cave, for there were too many things to observe. Of course, my attitude may have been coloured by the knowledge that I was the first person to be present at the nocturnal feasts of the *guacharos*.

# 6 *Snakes and bats*

Locations for filming wildlife provide many strange film sets. The background for the *guacharos* in the Diablotin and Oropuche Caves was a most distinguished setting but although it was satisfactory visually, it proved to be totally unsuitable for sound recordings. The roar of the water echoed among the steep walls in the caves and drowned all other sounds, including the clicking of the adults, their harsh screams and the whistling calls of the young.

John Dunston was familiar with the various oilbird caves and he advised trying the ones at Aripo. The entrance to these caves is by means of an almost vertical opening. It would have been impossible to find the entrance without the help of John and Raphael, a native guide, because it lies hidden in the rain-forest and one has to be practically on top of the opening before seeing it.

As the route through the rain-forest is long and the going extremely difficult we set out for the caves just before dawn. An expedition through forests in Sweden is a simple matter by comparison. There is nothing light-hearted about the rain-forest and one can sense the savagery all around. The rain-forest may look soft and luxuriant but there are sharp thorns that stab and leaves that have razor-like edges, and ants and various kinds of stinging insects proliferate.

It is worth cutting one's way through the vegetation carefully rather than hacking at it indiscriminately. Two tough lianas may well be joined together at a height of six to ten feet above the ground by a colony of angry bees. Bees do not like their peace disturbed and are quick to retaliate. They seem to fulfil the role of a police force in the jungle. Their stings are an effective weapon and a disturbed colony alerts other forms of animal life. I saw a remarkable example of how effectively the bees can protect other species. In the lower end of a creeper, hanging about six feet above the ground, there was a colony of bees the size of a croquet ball. Just above the colony and actually in contact with its roof was a very small bird's nest. The nest was round, with an opening at the side, and the bird flew out before I could identify it. The nest was well protected against predators. The slightest movement from a young opossum or a tree-snake with designs on the nest, and the police force would have gone into action.

There were mosquitoes everywhere. In books about the tropics one never reads about midges; mosquitoes sound much bigger, more objectionable and more venomous. I have often been asked whether I did not find the mosquitoes extremely tiresome, but in spite of their plague proportions they were nothing like as objectionable as the Swedish midges. In our mountains the bites from the armada of midges and biting flies are much more savage.

The route up the mountain where the Aripo caves are has the reputation of being a favourite place for snakes. Trinidad has 36 species but although only four of them are venomous the venom of these is extremely potent. All four are found within this area and I was excited by the prospect of finding some specimens. We had been going for about an hour on the slopes of Aripo when the boys in front of me began to jump about and shout: '*Mapipire, mapipire!*'

A small brown snake slithered across a brown carpet of fallen leaves and spun round to form a decorative coil, adopting the same posture as that of the European adder but doing it much faster. A fer-de-lance not longer than 15 inches put out its tongue at us, making use of Jacobson's organ to test the nature of the odours coming from the group of two-legged monsters. We were sweating so much after our steep climb that there was undoubtedly sufficient scent for the snake to identify us. This species has probably been named fer-de-lance on account of the speed with which it strikes. I was anxious to catch it and present it to the Butantan Institute at Sao Paolo in Brazil, which I hoped to visit later.

I decided to drink up most of the contents of my water-bottle and to empty out the rest, so that I could use the bottle as a container for the snake. After a lot of trouble I managed to get a grip on the back of the snake's neck. The small head was extremely active, twisting around ominously. Too much pressure applied to the neck is likely to damage a member of the viper family and in captivity they will not eat after such treatment. The whole operation was quite absorbing. The snake was not too keen on the bottle as a place of residence and struggled to slip free. I borrowed a shirt and wrapped it round the bottle, leaving only the neck free; I then held the bottle under my arm and bent down at a slight angle.

Next I held the snake still for a moment with its head near the bottle so that it could take scent from the neck. It was a risky procedure, but I believed the idea would work and so I released my grip on the snake. Its tongue tested the opening of the bottle. No strange scent had been left behind from the clean water and the snake could see the light shining through the bottom of the bottle. It glided forward into the neck and I quickly stuffed the rest of its body in. Before the snake could turn round I had put on the stopper which John had held ready. We then continued on our way, still climbing in the heat. Now and then we stopped, unscrewed the stopper and blew in air with a small battery-driven fan, which I intended to use in the cave to keep the humidity from the camera lenses.

The water which had been in the bottle was by no means irreplaceable. At various places along the route there were small runnels of clear, tolerably cool water which would have been of considerable interest to a freshwater biologist with a microscope. As far as drinking it was concerned, it was probably best to have been brought up on it from childhood like our friend Raphael.

As he dealt a strong blow which cut off a long liana which extended high above us in the darkness of the green forest, Raphael cried out: 'Water vine!' But no water ran out until he had cut off another

18-inch length, and then the flow started. The long cells in the wood retain their contents by capillary action until the upper halves of the cells have been removed. The liquid obtained from a liana of this length was sufficient to provide a whole glass of cell water which, like the best drinking water, had no taste. We worked hard, cutting our way through the rain-forest for about seven hours, and from time to time were able to refresh ourselves from the natural resources of the rain-forest.

The description of caves may seem tedious to people who have never been inside them but for those of us on the spot the Aripo cave was unquestionably exciting. There are really four caves, all lying within a limited area in the rolling forest which covers the slopes of Aripo. The rain-forest is often described as a green hell. The route is deadly monotonous but one of the reasons why Raphael was able to lead us so accurately was that local people still use the caves for harvesting the oilbirds. Raphael told us that the month of May was the time for taking the young birds. In the first cave, according to Snow, we expected to find ten birds but when we got there we could only find a single pair.

One of the other caves, according to Snow, should have contained eighty birds and as it was alleged to have a dry bottom, which would make it suitable for recording sounds free of disturbance, we decided to investigate it. I asked Raphael if it was also used for taking an annual crop but he explained that the cave was too dangerous.

When we got there I understood why. How the birds manœuvred in and out of such a place I do not know. We approached it via a long cave shaped like a slanting funnel. The walls were completely covered with layers of meditating scorpions. The ground was slippery with wet mud and bat droppings. This cave did not contain a single bird, but at the bottom end, between a couple of stone blocks, we found a small opening. This was the entrance to the cave we were seeking.

One by one we crept backwards down into a small chamber with a beautiful drapery of stalagmites and stalactites. In the confusion of stalagmites on the floor John found the entrance to the next chamber.

This was down another set of steps, three floors below ground level. As we groped our way down, accompanied by dancing lights, the birds were warned of our progress and we heard their angry protests below.

The going was treacherous and we had to get a careful grip on the calcareous growths and try to put our feet in the right place. Directly beneath the entrance there was another hole with slippery slopes which served as the run-off for all the water that gathers into this funnel during the rainy season. When I was well down among the birds I broke off a calcareous projection and let it fall to the 'fourth floor'. I never heard it arrive at the bottom, there was no thump or thud; this was probably because it had made a soft landing on a bottom embedded in bird and bat guano. If I had fallen through the outflow I would presumably have been engulfed eventually by the sludge.

In the story where the oilbirds were, the floor had the same consistency as the mud at Caroni: damp, loose guano with harder areas and a couple of calcareous ridges in the middle. We placed the tape-recorder on the floor and I was lucky enough to get very successful recordings of all the sounds made by the birds, as well as the whole chorus of song.

Raphael was decidedly relieved when we surfaced again as we were short of time for the return journey. The route which had taken us seven hours to cut on the way up had to be forced in less than two hours if we were not to spend the night in the rain-forest. It was as well to avoid this because all the unpleasant kinds of snake become active at night. In daylight there is practically no danger from the two species of coral-snake but after dark they are on the move. The bushmaster, which is called *Mapipire zananah* in the Trinidad patois and which may reach a length of ten feet, is found in this area but is difficult to spot in the dark with torches. *Zananah* means pineapple-coloured and in this kind of terrain its delicate yellowish-pink hue provides remarkably good protective coloration.

Finding our way back along the same route and looking out for the marks we had made on leaves and branches all took time. It is not an easy process in any event but becomes very much more difficult when it is pouring with rain. There was one night when we got drenched in heavy rain, our torches failed after a period in the wet, and we were forced to pick our way forward, trusting blindly in our instincts.

On this occasion, however, conditions were good. At one stage two of the boys suddenly half-jumped in front of me and one of them, Elliot, screamed and leaped into the air with his feet wide apart. He had been lucky, for he had trodden with his feet on either side of a coiled fer-de-lance, which lay with its tail rustling in the leaves like a rattlesnake. It waves its tail like some other South American snakes but it does not have a rattle like the related rattlesnake.

This specimen was large, about 55 inches long. Although Elliot had obviously received a fright, he insisted on catching the snake himself. His legs were trembling but all went well. After capturing it safely, he marched at the head of our party, triumphantly holding it aloft. We reached the small path from which we had started just before darkness fell. There we were met by a Negro with very curly yellowish-white hair who had just killed an even bigger specimen. He had cut it in front of the anus and the eggs of the gravid female were hanging out.

At the virus laboratory in Port of Spain I managed to obtain some laboratory white mice to feed my two fer-de-lance specimens. When I said what I wanted them for the staff shook their heads and reminded me that Beebe had never managed to get the fer-de-lance to feed. I had read about the investigations in the Bronx Zoo in New York, where it was successfully established that the bushmaster can only be kept in good condition, with a healthy appetite, at a temperature a little below 20°C (68°F)—which is the same temperature as the relatively cool nights in the mountain districts of Trinidad. I placed the snakes in a cool, air-conditioned place and waited a couple of days. Then, as soon as the smallest of the two snakes was offered a mouse, it ate it. I timed it with a stop watch and reckoned that from the moment of the strike the mouse lived exactly fifteen seconds.

Many people consider it distasteful to offer live food to a snake, but compared with the death a laboratory mouse can expect, quick death by venom is preferable. As these particular specimens of fer-de-lance were needed to help research in Butantan for the preparation of anti-venine serum, it was essential that they should feed and arrive in good condition. Providing that they reached Dr Hoge at the Institute, they would stand every chance of living a healthy life.

The fast action of the venom certainly aroused my respect and made me more willing to believe a story previously told me by an Indian. His father had gone out one night to hunt illegally with a torch. In the beam of light he saw the reflection of a pair of eyes. It was an opossum, or manicou as it is called in Trinidad, a species that is popular as prey. The animal disappeared into a hole in a tree-trunk. The man enlarged the hole with his knife and stabbed downwards to kill the opossum. The rest of the story was based on surmise as the man had gone out alone and no one was there to witness subsequent events. Later he was found dead at the foot of the tree—and inside the hole in the tree were a venom-killed manicou and a decidedly active fer-de-lance.

I met another Indian who had been bitten in the foot. He had reached the hospital in Port of Spain in time and had recovered, but it was not until two months later that he was fit to resume work. Several snakes belonging to the same group as the fer-de-lance are considered to have extremely fast-working venom. A puff adder has been known to kill a man in about two minutes. A bite from a snake with blood-coagulating venom, made for example in the veins of a man's lower arm, may result in a blood clot which travels quickly towards the heart or which may simply form in the blood vessels.

Later on when I visited the Butantan Snake Institute they told me that the fer-de-lance is the species which strikes the hardest. The fangs will even penetrate leather boots. In Trinidad the fer-de-lance is called *Mapipire balsain* (basin snake), since it likes damp places with small runnels, precisely the type of terrain found over the whole of the northern mountain range. A plantation owner told me that when he cleared new ground they had killed 31 *Mapipire* in one area. I asked him to let me know if he found any *Mapipire zananah*. However hard I searched I never succeeded in finding a bushmaster. The plantation owner never got in touch with me, and although I offered 25 dollars for a live *zananah*, none of the mountain dwellers ever claimed the reward. This snake is greatly feared. Its length is sufficiently impressive in itself and the amount of venom is in proportion to its size. Professor Wolfgang Bucherl in Butantan, however, states that the venom of the bushmaster is among the less active; the fer-de-lance is decidedly more venomous.

When the mountain people of Trinidad see a snake their reaction is unequivocal: a quick blow and the snake is dead, venomous or no. John Dunston had already earned the reputation of being possessed by the devil because he handled snakes and climbed about in caves. It was not long before I had a similar reputation. One day when we were out together we met an old man on a small path. The old man stopped and stared. He had a white beard and a small hole appeared in it as his jaw dropped. Perhaps this was not so surprising because decoratively draped over John's arm was a nine-foot long boa, *Constrictor constrictor*, one of the six species which snake-experts reckon among the giant snakes. John had bought it for five dollars and, as was typical of his good nature, he was going to release it. To reassure the old man he explained that he had recited certain incantations over the snake and it was now completely harmless. Superstition is unbelievably rife in connection with many aspects of life in Trinidad. For instance, it is said that if a woman eats two fused bananas she will have twins. I also saw evidence of an extraordinary degree of credibility from reading Trinidad's newspaper, the *Sunday Mirror*. In the issue of 10th October, 1965, the whole of the front page was taken up with a feature about three women who claimed to have been bitten by witches. Descriptions of their experiences were accompanied by a two-column picture of each woman.

'When I awoke this morning I felt very weak,' complained one of them, 'and one of my legs felt sore. I could not understand why, but when I looked at my leg I saw a dark blue mark and there were several tooth marks around it. I was scared stiff when I realised that my blood had been sucked by a *soucouyant.*'

One of the other victims reported: 'Often when I go to look at the corn at night I see a big fire-ball moving across the sky.'

The newspaper added the following footnote: 'A *soucouyant* is Trinidad's equivalent of a European witch. It may be an old woman in a village who has inherited some of the black magic art, who can change her form and become a fire-ball, flying around at night seeking victims.' This was actually printed in a newspaper in October, 1965!

The correct explanation of the marks of the bite on the woman lay in the nocturnal visits of a vampire bat, *Desmodus rotundus rotundus*. Strictly speaking this is a more frightening alternative than an old woman playing at being a combination of satellite and witch. The vampires can, in fact, spread rabies, which is often a fatal disease. One of the duties of the staff of the virus laboratory was to collect vampires and kill them. This is a colossal task since these animals spend the day in a variety of places including caves, houses, hollow trees, old cellars and so on. However one year they managed to collect 1,800 specimens and on one occasion 500 vampires were taken in a single locality. A vampire will drink nearly sixty grams of blood per night.

Accordingly it has been reckoned that this annual catch represents a saving of almost 40,000 litres of blood per year, primarily of course from cattle.

It is understandable that people should regard the visits of vampires as supernatural. In one house the same person may, in fact, be attacked time after time while others, sleeping even in the same room, are never bitten. Moreover the attacks take place without the victim waking up at all. The vampire's razor-sharp teeth make a completely painless incision; an efficient suction tube is formed by the underside of the tongue and a deep groove in the lower lip. The vampire sucks so much blood that it is often incapable of flying but staggers away from its private drinking orgy on all fours. It is expert in this method of progression and with its body raised up it can move quite fast. The action is jerky but it is a form of adaptation which is practical and expedient. Victims may be bitten anywhere: on the fingers, toes, nose, ears, and now and again on the lips. The latter is particularly distasteful when one remembers that cattle are often bitten by vampires in the anal region.

If the blood donors are involuntary the vampire's preference for a particular individual is very marked, even if difficult to explain. Of fifty police horses in Port of Spain only one was attacked every night for a week.

It is not only *Desmodus* that can transmit rabies. There is another blood-sucking bat, *Diaemus*, which mostly attacks birds. In addition there are three insectivorous and three fruit-eating species which have been proved to carry this dreaded virus. Among the latter was the fruit-eating *Carollia*, which frequently alighted on us in the bat caves. While I was looking for oilbirds in Diablotin Cave with the infra-red viewer, I often saw bats fluttering and was subjected to a form of Chinese torture by a group of *Carollia* bats on the roof of the chamber as they dripped 'water' on me at irregular intervals.

There was a donkey which lived about 300 yards from the mouth of the cave and was bitten every night by a vampire bat: I hoped to film the bat in the act of sucking the donkey's blood but the donkey died before I could carry out my plans. As for myself, although I expected to become a target for a vampire at some time or other, in fact I was never bitten. Only sleeping individuals are attacked, and knowledge of this helped to keep me awake during the long periods when I was waiting in the caves for the adult oilbirds to return to feed

*Tobago is probably the island Daniel Defoe had in mind when he wrote* Robinson Crusoe. *With its temperature of 25-27°C (77-80°F) in the shade, coral-reefs off the long sandy beaches, and coconut palms and rain-forest up the slopes, Crusoe was indeed fortunate.*

their young. The monotonous sound of the water in the cave was extremely conducive to sleep and when I lay flat on my stomach on the platform, ready to take pictures of a nest below, I often dropped off to sleep. I tend to do this when waiting to film, as for instance during long periods of inactivity at the nests of goshawk and other species in Sweden. One night in the cave I thought I felt something running across my back; I might have been dreaming but it was the same sensation as when a bird-eating spider climbs over you. I woke up with a start and immediately the sensation was gone. It may have been a subconscious warning. On the other hand, if it really was a vampire, it is possible that it was not interested in the blood of a diabetic.

Remarkably enough the bat which bears the scientific name *Vampyrum spectrum* does not suck blood at all. The species is known as the great false vampire. With its wing-span of 2½ feet it looks quite gruesome. It feeds on birds and small mammals and now and again also catches other species of bat.

All in all the research worker interested in bats has a varied field of study in Trinidad. Amongst other things, Don Griffin and his co-workers have investigated the technique of fishing in the fish-eating bat, *Noctilio leporinus*. The United States Air Force is said to have been very interested in learning how this bat, using echo-location, can detect the position of a fish under the water. It is difficult to estimate the exact position of a visible object under the surface of clear water on account of refraction and with ordinary echo-location this should be impossible. It was shown quite clearly by the investigations of Griffin and his co-worker Rod Suthers at Simla that the fish-eating

ABOVE *West Indian flamingoes in flight: in the background, a long pink line of thousands of long-legged and long-necked members of the same species searching for food.* BELOW *This species of flamingo is very tall. With head down in the water it filters its food (small organisms) with its peculiar beak. As can be seen, the lower half of the beak is larger than the upper half.*

bat only takes objects at the surface of the water and that their signals therefore function in one medium only.

These small mammals can be seen fishing amongst pelicans before the sun sets. Small fry are alarmed at the presence of the pelicans and scatter in all directions; the pelicans make sudden plunging dives straight into the water and flounder about on the surface, dipping the whole bill right into the water. Pelicans thus make useful companions for the fish-eating bats, which sweep along close above the water surface, advancing on a fish and seizing it by the ridge on its back, gripping it with the long claws of their back legs. As they fly on there is an audible crunching as the small fish are eaten. In the hollow trees where these bats spend their period of rest the fish scales often form a silvery trail at the entrance and lead right into the tree. There is a strong aroma round the whole silvery abode.

Trinidad is known as the island of hummingbirds. Sixteen species of these small nectar-sipping birds occur there. When they go to rest at night and become inactive, their place is taken by a nectar-sipping bat, *Anoura geoffroyi*, which not unexpectedly has certain features in common with its feathered colleagues. It can hover in front of a flower and its extremely long tongue functions like a fuel pump. The tongue is longer, in fact, than the whole bat.

All these animals that live in the shadows are only part of the incomparably rich nocturnal fauna in Trinidad. As in Sweden even the other mammals are most active during the hours of darkness. For me these hours are particularly stimulating as one's senses are on the alert. Unable to see as well in the dark, one has to listen with acute concentration, mentally tuned to interpreting what one hears, and often one's sense of smell seems to become astonishingly sharper. Under these conditions the way of life of our ancestors seems not so remote and one gets a glimpse of how they must have adapted themselves to a more primitive existence. Living close to other living beings seems to me to be the right way of life.

# 7 *Children of the rain-forest*

If one could hear every signal sent out in the dark by the bats all along the northern range of mountains in Trinidad, the noise would be like the bedlam in a bird house at the zoo. Instead, with the continuous murmuring and chirping of thousands of insects, it all sounds very peaceful. There are sporadic interjections from the gentle pinging voice of a frog, *Eleutherodactylus wrichi*, and superimposed on this general background of sound are the long-drawn-out notes of a distant potoo. 'Po-po-po-po-po-poo' resounds through the darkness as male screech owls call from all directions. Their notes are somewhat reminiscent of Tengmalm's owl although the rhythm is different. Another sound which can be heard, like a roll of drums on a tree-trunk, is made by the spectacled owl as it marks its territory by calling from the giant trees in the rain-forest.

Considering the amount of rain which falls in the mountains the numbers of amphibians are not as great as one might expect. Near the quieter parts of streams, however, one can hear two voices carrying on a conversation: 'Work, work' says *Hyla maxima*, a large tree-frog, and back comes the reply '*Oui, oui, oui*' from the small *Leptodactylus typhonius*. The real paradise of the amphibians, however, is down in the low-lying swampy regions. One place where the chorus of small pumping frogs and toads is almost deafening is Nariva Swamp. The Latin names of these amphibians do not tell us much about their voices but my own field notes are much more helpful. The names I wrote down are suggestive of the rich instrumentation of an amphibian orchestra. The performers included the following:

Bzzz, klick-pling, clang, scream, whimper, castanet, woodpecker, empty bottles, door-bell, owl echo—and many others.

Quite the most beautiful composition comes from the gigantic *Bufo marinus*, a species which qualifies as a competitor with *Bufo blombergi* for the title of 'the world's largest toad.'

There was a small pool where several males often sang together, making a melodic humming with a series of long-drawn-out notes. One toad after another takes up the tune. When I imitated the sound, there was a splash and an incensed baritone swam quickly towards me, popped out on to a stone and distending his imposing throat sac delivered his answer, 'Arrrrr!'

Dawn comes quickly as in all tropical regions, and for those who are prepared both to listen and to watch, the heights in the northern range of mountains offer a grandstand view. The ball of the sun comes up over the horizon and climbs into the sky, lighting up the bright red immortelle blooms and making them glow against the dark green forest.

A short burst of vibrating calls from a tinamou soon dies down, only to be followed by the powerful chorus of sound from the song birds, each one advertising the fact that it has taken up residence and is available for mating in its private retreat. The change from the night sky to the sharply delineated contours as the sun comes up takes place remarkably quickly. There is a glow of red, as red as the scarlet ibises, which comes from the masses of flowers; the red seems to rise up almost from the ground. This is the favourite colour of the nectar-sipping hummingbirds, which also visit the yellow *poui* and the brilliant crowns of pink *poui* in the flower gardens.

The warm colour tones of the immortelle flowers look gloriously rich against the blue sky. In some of the tall straight trees, the whole crown appears to be full of hanging baskets looking like pendulous fruits among the red blooms. Birds that are yellow and black, quite large and with blue eyes, fly in and out of the tops of the baskets, some of them busily building a new nest. These are the female yellowtails which bear the full responsibility for caring for the young, including the building of the slender nest, which is normally about $4\frac{1}{2}$ feet long. If the nest-building takes place during a couple of windy, rainy days, as often occurs at the start of the dry season, it will become stretched to double this length or more.

The males appear to be quite unconcerned and play no part in nest-building but devote themselves to song and courtship, particularly the latter, for this species is polygamous and the male distributes his favours among several females. The display song always takes place accompanied by a characteristic exhibition of gymnastics. The male bends well forward over a branch, spreads the tail-feathers over his back, turns his wings outwards and backwards, and vibrates them. This produces a rustling sound and throughout the display he gives piercing but quite tuneful calls. The male often flies straight to a nest and displays immediately in front of the female and then flies on to the next nest where there is a female and repeats the performance.

When the rays of the sun penetrate farther down the slopes they fall on yet another brilliant sight. The upperparts are a flashing, metallic green and the underparts are orange. This bird, the size of a song thrush, is a jacamar and it has a long, thin, slightly curved bill. A museum specimen seems decidedly gaudy but in its own surroundings in the rain-forest it is very difficult to spot; the metallic sheen serves as an excellent camouflage.

It is most easily seen from April to June along the high banks where pairs of jacamar excavate nest tunnels. The burrow is about fifteen inches long, and ends in a nest chamber. It is charming to watch the male offering the female a brightly coloured butterfly, for the male is slightly smaller than the female. She can be recognised by the colour of her throat, which is, unlike that of the male, not white but a pale buff. As frequently happens all over the world, the way to the heart is through the stomach, and the female is often fed by the male while taking her share in digging out the burrow.

Also along the banks, in the same steep walls of mud, a larger hole may be found. By shouting a subdued 'ho,' one can get a reply from the hole quite quickly. With a little persistence and luck, a motmot eventually comes out to drive away the supposed rival by a long series of territorial calls. Having roused the bird it is not easy to stop it scolding at you but this hardly matters when you can enjoy the sight of an apparition in pale green, with broad blue-green eyebrows, red-brown eyes and a long blue tail, in which the two longest feathers carry a small flag at the end, separated from the rest of the vane by a bare section. Amongst motmot experts there is still some controversy as to whether the missing area of feather vane falls off of its own accord or whether the motmot removes it deliberately.

The black-and-white manakins lack iridescence. On the other hand, their appearance is particularly striking. The major part of every day is spent by the males in waiting for the females, guarding a display arena and removing leaves and twigs from it. The arena is usually a small area on the floor of the forest between two saplings. Now and again the males shake their wings with a peculiar loud rustling and give out a 'tjerr' call. It is all rather peaceful until a female arrives in the vicinity. The male then gives a whistling call to attract the female and courtship starts in earnest. This involves the male flying backwards and forwards between the display perches; his throat is distended and loud snapping sounds come from the bill. These are reminiscent of a toy pistol. One is reminded of the traditional scene in a western film when the entry of Texas Rose into the saloon is greeted by shouts and whistles, and shots are fired.

Manakins are very entertaining to watch, specially the blue-backed manakin whose song I had the good fortune to record in Tobago. Strangely enough this species is not found in Trinidad, although it is abundant in Venezuela. A joint dance is performed by two males, and the display starts as soon as two males meet. It is not an aggressive performance; on the contrary it looks more like two small urchins playing leap-frog. The males have a deep blue patch on the back and the two performers start a rhythmic whining sound which might well be the envy of some of today's pop-singers. The males hop up and down on a branch in a tree, making their metallic mechanical sounds. The rhythm changes and the males start their leap-frogging.

While the one hops over the other the latter trips along a few steps, so that their leap-frogging continues in the same place all the time. It has to be seen to be appreciated and one wonders what function it serves.

The black-and-white manakin's pistol shot is a remarkably loud snapping sound, but the result produced is not nearly as impressive as the sound made by the bell-bird. The latter is remarkably like a hammer blow on a church bell or even on a long metal tube. Dr Schneirla of the American Museum of Natural History in New York has told how he once went wandering off for a walk in Trinidad and ill-advisedly failed to take his bush-knife and compass with him. As he wandered in the southern part of the island he could hear workmen busily laying an oil pipe-line in the ground and made sure to keep them within earshot. Later, in the afternoon, he decided to make his way leisurely towards them; he could still hear them busily at work, now and again delivering a series of blows as they adjusted sections of the piping. Eventually he realised that for the last hour bell-birds had been playing at pipe-laying and he had lost his way. This can be very dangerous in such terrain. If one can find a stream there is a chance of following it as a guide, but I have heard of a group of hunters who got lost for six days in the dense forest belt in the Aripo region, in the same area where our trips to the oilbird caves took place.

The streams provide the only chance of seeing mammals during the daytime in places where there is sufficient light for photography. In the forest itself, even when a ray of sunshine penetrates through the foliage, the light is so weak that even the fastest lenses cannot give a satisfactory exposure on the colour film with which I was working. The streams provide long slits in the green Venetian blinds of the forest and the ripple of the water drowns the hum of the camera as the deer approach. The brocket deer which is found in Trinidad looks rather like the European roe deer, although it does not belong to the same genus; it is smaller and fox-red in colour. About two foot high at the shoulders, which are rounded, it is perfectly adapted to moving through the dense, hanging vegetation.

To describe the rain-forest as dangerous is an understatement: it can be lethal in places. This is not because of the danger from snakes, nor is it due to the presence of puma or jaguar, neither of which occurs in Trinidad. The real danger arises from the presence of the brocket deer.

A tame European roe deer can be dangerous because the antlers are extremely sharp and an imprinted roebuck attacks every human since it is simply defending its territory against rivals. It is not this kind of danger which lurks along the tracks of the brocket in Trinidad. The people hunt to kill and killing is done by the simplest and most effective method. Several protected areas exist on paper and certain methods of hunting are forbidden, but the local people either do not know much about these regulations or simply choose to ignore them.

One method of hunting which is forbidden is as follows. The hunter finds a well-used brocket path and installs a simple but gruesomely effective trap. A tube filled with scrap-iron and gunpowder, fitted with a fuse cap, is directed at the path; a thin cord is stretched across the path, attached to a branch on the opposite side, and connected with an ordinary rat-trap. When the brocket comes along the path, the cord releases the striking mechanism of the rat-trap, which hits the fuse cap, and the scrap-iron in the tube is expelled into the body of the brocket—or of the person who happens to be unsuspectingly walking along the path.

The irresponsible and indiscriminate hunting of everything that moves has resulted in a dearth of animals in the areas close to settlements and roads. Regulations regarding protected species are not effective and during my stay in Trinidad an ocelot was shot. This is one of the protected species and was one of the last specimens on the island. The paca, a rodent the size of a small pig, has become very rare in Trinidad. This attractive animal with white spots on its sides is similar in appearance to a brocket fawn; it can swim and dive well and mainly feeds on land. The only huntable mammal that appears to be able to survive satisfactorily on the island is the agouti, a rodent the size of a hare but which looks more like a long-legged brown guinea-pig. The agouti and paca are the staple food of a large aquatic reptile, the anaconda, which I had the luck to film on two different occasions.

Recorded measurements of the length of this giant snake are the subject of a great deal of controversy. The prepared skins of giant snakes are unsatisfactory as evidence because they can be stretched considerably. After preparation and stretching, measurements of both the length and breadth are very misleading. The most reliable method is to catch the snake alive and measure it before it is killed. This was successfully demonstrated by Rolf Blomberg in the film *Anaconda*, in which he and his four assistants were seen capturing a 21-foot specimen after a struggle. The greatest length so far recorded is 37 feet. This is quoted by the American herpetologist Clifford H. Pope, and the measurements were recorded by a geologist in Colombia. If these measurements were correct the anaconda is not only the thickest but also the longest of all snakes.

The name anaconda is not in current use everywhere in Brazil; it is usually known there as the *sucuri*. In Trinidad and Guyana the name anaconda is widely used, probably because visiting zoologists are mainly British or American. It appears to originate in India, and a large part of the populations of this region are Indian. In Tamil there is a word, *anai*, which means elephant, and another, *kolra*, which means killer. Fusion of the words would have applied just as well to the 18-foot Indian python, *Python molurus*, as to the sucuri of South America. In Trinidad the anaconda is also known locally, probably by people of Carib origin, as *huilla* or *whilla*.

Just before I arrived on the island a large specimen had been killed. I was told about it by Mike Emsley, who has written a scientific paper on Trinidad's snake fauna. This anaconda was twenty-seven feet long. Two people who have seen most of the reptile fauna of Trinidad are Hans and Julius Boos. They are brothers; both are keenly interested in snakes and they took me to a small river to try to get pictures of the anaconda. Although it was still the rainy season, the weather had been dry for some days and as a result the water in the river was clear and unclouded. On rainy days this kind of stream soon becomes yellowish-brown with all the mud that is carried down in it.

Everything was therefore auspicious for filming the beautiful greenish snake with its large dark rings. We found a specimen on a dead tree-trunk immediately above the stream. The anaconda, which was approximately between 12 and 15 feet long, appeared not to notice our arrival and certainly showed no obvious interest in us. It is possible that it had recently swallowed some prey, but no large bulge was visible in it. It flicked its tongue a little listlessly, lowered its head towards the water, glided a foot or two forward and then stopped.

An anaconda of this size has no true enemies, at least not on this island, where there are no big cats larger than an ocelot. But if hunters armed with machetes happen to meet this large 'dragon' they naturally hack it to pieces. They do exactly the same to small non-venomous snakes, reacting instinctively to all snakes in the same way, just as Europeans will tremble with fright and set about a harmless grass-snake with a stick.

The stream was fairly shallow and as I wanted to film this *huilla* in the water I went to a sunny place farther downstream. The water came only just above my knees. I reckoned that when the snake came down from the tree-trunk it would follow the run of the stream, and so I would be in a position to get a sequence of it moving past me. I shouted to my companions, who drove the anaconda down from its resting place. Everything went according to plan. The camera was already running as the snake came towards me. I was standing against the light and I must have looked like a small misshapen tree. The snake accordingly treated me like a tree-trunk and pressed against me, using my thigh as a support before it shot between my legs and continued on at good speed. The camera recorded the whole manœuvre and the results gave me some of the more unusual picture angles obtained during the year.

The snake was not at all difficult to manage after this incident and we were able to halt its progress by leaping round it and splashing, enabling me to film it from all possible angles. I wonder whether the anaconda's evil reputation is not coloured by the murderous reaction which it seems to arouse instinctively in *Homo sapiens* and other apes.

On the other occasion when I managed to film the anaconda, I went right under the water in an effort to get new camera angles. As before, I chose a suitable place and the anaconda was chased away, higher upstream, while I got into position with the underwater camera. It glided towards the place where I had positioned myself, and came to rest quickly on the surface of the water above a deep pool which had been formed by the stream.

Standing on some rocks in the middle, I held the camera above my head and lowered it into position. I started filming the snake from above, then with the camera still running sank down under the water and swam towards the coils of the snake. The anaconda shot away and I swam after it. It was one of the most fascinating moments I have ever experienced and I relive it every time I see the film. In Kipling's *Jungle Book*, Mowgli swims with Kaa, the big reticulated python, friend and protector of the small human. I was thinking of this while watching the thickset but supple body of the snake, meandering gently and weightlessly through the water. Through the camera view-finder its muscular body gave a formidable impression of controlled power. But it was only when I saw the film at home in Sweden that I noticed for the first time how very long the anaconda looked. There had been no tape measure ready-to-hand underwater and I shall never know its precise measurements.

# 8 *The luck of Robinson Crusoe*

It is thought that when Daniel Defoe wrote *Robinson Crusoe* he had Trinidad's neighbouring island Tobago in mind. It has been suggested that the idea for the book was based on the experiences of the Scots sailor, Alexander Selkirk, who lived on the island of Juan Fernandez, off Chile. Whether or not Defoe stole the idea from Selkirk is a matter of opinion, but there is no doubt that as an island, Tobago has pride of place since it is just the kind of island where a shipwrecked man could make himself at home and live under conditions that not only ensured his survival but are more akin to paradise.

The flora is luxuriant, everything grows in abundance and although the rain-forest is present, it is neither as rampant as in Trinidad nor as extensive. Tobago is only one-seventh the size of Trinidad. Every kind of fruit-bearing and decorative flowering species capable of growing in a tropical environment seems to have been introduced and become established here. The first true colonisation of the island took place in the year 1616.

There are few mammals in Tobago, even fewer than in Trinidad. Red brocket deer, nine-banded armadillo, opossum, agouti, squirrel, seven species of rats and mice, together with seventeen bats, make up Tobago's total list of mammal species. There are fewer species of birds than in Trinidad but still a rich variety. Several species not to be found in Trinidad occur in Tobago, amongst others the red-tailed guan or chachalaca, which is almost the size of a turkey. In spite of persistent persecution it can still often be heard calling loudly in a chorus that sounds like 'Chachalaca, chachalaca, chachalaca . . .'

The beaches in Tobago are extremely beautiful. There are gently curving bays fringed with palms where the lazy ripple of the water provides a soft rhythmic background music that is soothing and peaceful, washing away the troubles of yesterday and today. The sun sparkles on the water, which is pale green over the coral-reefs and steel-blue farther out; the air is filled with the scents of the rain-forest and the tang of the salt from the sea. These are the same beaches, indolent and beautiful, which in the past witnessed some of the bloodiest fights that have ever taken place on any island.

The history of Tobago is steeped in violence, for the island was tossed to and fro by the colonial powers like a ball in a game. Since the beginning of the seventeenth century, it has been governed by the following in chronological order. In 1616, colonists from Barbados were eaten up by Caribs and the same fate met two hundred Dutchmen and their families. Thereupon Holland took possession of the island. In 1666 the English defeated the Dutch and their French allies at Bloody Bay. But British rule was short-lived in Tobago, and in the same year it was taken over by free-booters from Jamaica who were forced, however, to surrender to French colleagues from Grenada. The French in their turn were driven away by the Dutch. Then the British returned, followed by the Dutch, and then the French once again held the island for a time until the British re-occupied it. After a period of being tossed backwards and forwards between France and England, Tobago finally ended up under the British flag in 1814. In 1962 Tobago was given her independence as part of the state of Trinidad and Tobago.

One of the reasons for the fierceness of the struggle for Tobago is the island's fertility. In addition the climate is good and Tobago is usually spared by the hurricanes which frequently strike the chain of West Indian islands. Moreover, it has a large, sheltered natural harbour called Man-o-War Bay, a name which in the circumstances was particularly appropriate. This harbour had considerable naval importance because of its key position at a time when piracy was very profitable.

Today a different kind of invasion takes place. Every year from December to June wave after wave of tourists stream on to the island, although there are still plenty of lonely palm beaches where one can play at being Robinson Crusoe, with flocks of parrots screaming among the clusters of palm trees and Robinsonian goats bleating on the slopes. Canadians seem to be particularly taken with the island, and rightly so. I met one who, of all the West Indian islands, preferred Tobago for his holidays, staying at a small hotel at the farthest point from the capital Scarborough, called Bird of Paradise Inn. This lies immediately opposite the island of Little Tobago, also known as Bird of Paradise Island, which is the only place outside Australia, New Guinea, and certain islands in their vicinity where one can see and hear birds of paradise.

The introduction of the greater bird of paradise, *Paradisea apoda*, took place in 1909. At that time the fashion of wearing feathers as decorative adornments was at its height, a habit which the women of the western world shared with the Papuans in the mountain districts of New Guinea. In the case of the Papuans, however, the consumption was kept within certain limits. The desires of western women extended to the brilliant plumes of small hummingbirds as well as to the plumage remains of various species of bird of paradise. As a result these birds, which were first named by Linnaeus, were shot in such quantities that many species were soon on the verge of extinction.

A wealthy Englishman, Sir William Ingram, then had the far-sighted idea of saving the birds of paradise for posterity. He bought Little Tobago and equipped an expedition to the Aru Islands, off what was then Dutch New Guinea, where forty-seven specimens of this bird were caught. These were then released on Bird of Paradise Island, as Little Tobago came to be called.

I reckoned that the best time for filming and tape-recording the birds was during the period of pair formation when the males would be showing off to advantage. At Sten Bergmann's place in Rönninge I had had the pleasure of listening to and recording his birds of paradise, including *Paradisea minor*, a species which looks rather like the birds Sir William Ingram had formerly released on his island. I successfully obtained clear recordings of loud bird calls on this island; shrill screams could be heard everywhere reminiscent of poultry farms in Sweden. I also recorded feral cocks and hens, although these were interrupted now and again by the three or perhaps four or five birds of paradise still remaining on Little Tobago. (These are the last specimens there.) I had read Dr Gilliard's report on the investigation he made in 1958 on the island and was familiar with the fact that the descendants of the birds introduced in 1909 were then approximately 35 in number.

As I have mentioned, Tobago has for long been spared hurricanes —with one striking exception. In 1963, without warning of any kind, Hurricane Flora passed over Tobago and struck it so violently that whole coconut trees were snapped as though a giant had squashed them with his foot. A house with eight people inside was plucked up and whirled into the air. At 40 to 50 feet above the ground the roof was torn off but the rest of the house landed in the middle of a road without anyone being hurt. The vegetation on the island was destroyed to such an extent that it will take several decades for it to recover fully. The largest of the rain-forest trees were torn down, and on Little Tobago, where vegetation is sparse, less than ten birds of paradise remained after the hurricane. The others were blown out to sea.

It would have been easy to film the surviving males during their display. The display arena was conveniently in a place where the light was adequate but I was not prepared to risk disturbing the birds in the breeding season. If the stock is to re-establish itself every care must be taken not to interfere with them.

Strictly speaking the island is not entirely suited to these birds, which normally live in the rain-forest. So that adequate water is kept available for them, rain is collected during the rainy season in a large cistern, with the help of a specially constructed roof. The man who watches over the island, Jeremiah George, gives the birds water and food every morning and shoots any birds of prey which appear now and again. Without these protective measures the birds of paradise would have disappeared long ago.

Tobago has another zoological attraction: Buccoo Reef, world-famous for its rich marine animal life, and now heavily exploited by tourists. To visit Tobago without driving out to the reef is like going to Paris without seeing the Eiffel Tower. At a depth of only three feet there is an abundance of extremely colourful fishes. One of the local people who exploits the possibilities of the reef is Bill Craig, a professional frogman who for many years has dived all round Tobago and whose very expression betrays a taste for adventure. Bill was very interested in my Paillard camera with its underwater casing; he had filmed a great deal with another type of equipment but for some reason was not satisfied with it. I offered to lend him mine in exchange for his services as a guide to the best places on Buccoo Reef.

Bill told me of an incident which took place when he was using up his last roll of film. If luck had not been with him it could well have been the last picture he was ever to take. He was at a depth of about 30 feet, quietly looking for subjects to film, when he suddenly saw a shark approaching straight as an arrow towards him. It was probably attracted both by the sound of breathing from the aqualung and by the slight noise of the camera. Its eyes were placed so far out to the sides of its head that it could not see very well straight in front. Bill took refuge behind a pillar of coral, then in self-defence struck the shark on the nose with the full force of his camera. The shark reacted violently and instantly struck back.

*On St Giles large numbers of boobies and terns nest among the dense growth of cacti.*

Again and again it attacked until the blood flowed in dark clouds from its jaws. Fortunately it was the shark's own blood, for it was assailing the pillar of coral against which Bill had positioned the camera and from which he was now taking shots. Finally it swam away with bits of flesh and blood swirling in its tracks.

Bill also reported that he had once seen a monster of such huge dimensions and astonishing appearance that even he had been, in his own words, 'damned frightened.' He had a harpoon with him at the time as his intention was to shoot a sea-perch. He moved carefully round a wall of coral and came face to face with a gruesome animal that had a head like that of a 'prehistoric dinosaur'. Only a yard away he was confronted with a specimen of the leatherback turtle, an animal which may weigh more than half a ton. They stared at each other. The turtle was just as frightened as he was (a man in a diver's suit producing bubbles also looks rather weird) and started to paddle away fast. According to Bill, as the turtle started to move off it looked like a large motor-boat getting under way. This probably makes Bill the only person to meet the world's largest turtle underwater. One specimen of this rare animal was seen to go ashore fairly recently in Tobago. This is an unusual occurrence; on the other hand, the majority of the leatherback turtles go ashore to lay on the east coast of Trinidad which lies in the western part of the species' range. More will be said of this later.

I went out to the reef in Bill's boat, a craft which would impress even an astronaut, and it took us no time at all to get to a part of the reef where Bill promised barracudas. To my surprise both the barracudas and other fish were extremely shy and never came close enough for filming. I spent five days in all doing test dives in other places off the shores of Tobago but never had the chance to film any-

*Soon after hatching the young flamingoes assemble in flocks. At the end of May they leave Bonaire on a course towards Venezuela but eventually return there to nest.*

thing underwater. Eventually, off Arnos Vale, a hotel whose owner did not allow harpoon fishing in his territory, I found that the fish were tame enough to approach.

The reason why the marine life showed such fear of man in most of this area seems to be the usual one—irresponsible hunting. Underwater hunting has become the big attraction for people on holiday and diving is now common around all the accessible reefs. According to Bill, at one time Buccoo Reef was threatened but it has now been declared a protected area and hunting with harpoons is forbidden.

My wife, Camilla, had just joined me, and together we stayed at the Bird of Paradise Inn where the owner, Mr Lau, promised to arrange for boats to take me over to the rocky island of St Giles, the second of the two islands off Tobago in which I was interested. The first island is associated, by its name, with paradise but the second, St Giles, should by rights be associated with the other end of the scale. It has no water and the vegetation is a tangle of growth. Cacti of various sizes are closely mixed with six-foot high grass, and the whole area is interspersed with an extremely tough type of black bush. The place would be particularly suitable as a training ground for fakirs. The island is like a fortress, rising abruptly out of the sea and virtually impregnable except on one side of the coast. There is an area about six feet across where a boat can be taken in, providing the wind is in the right direction and the succession of waves is judged correctly.

One of the people who appreciated this inhospitable island was Bill Craig. In his view the undisturbed waters were good for both barracudas and sharks. The wealth of marine predators around the island is due to the large numbers of birds present on the fortress. There are boobies, frigate birds, gulls, terns and shearwaters, as well as many other smaller species. A number of the young fall into the sea, in some cases already dead from the heat of the sun. Once in the water they are quickly killed by the sharks.

Diving in this area is extremely dangerous and to fall in is even more risky. The German biologist Eibl-Eibesfeldt tells in his book on the Galapagos Islands of how he and Hans Hass had to protect themselves on a very similar coast with long sticks when they were attacked by three sharks. These 'free-booters of the sea' reckon that everything which comes along can be claimed as tribute. I had evidence of the presence of barracudas in the waters around Tobago because the crew in the boat pulled out two on the way over to St Giles.

We took two boats, one a powerful motor-boat, the other a small rowing-boat. There were five men available to help me land with the equipment. I took a lot of film on the way over as we tossed about in the passage between the high rock cliffs. Foaming waves dashed vertically against the bastions of rock. The wind was really bad and we were forced to sail backwards and forwards with only an occasional glimpse of the six-foot long beach between the heaving seas. The accompanying boat set out with two men on board and soon disappeared, riding the swell in the green water. Every now and again a column of rock suddenly appeared to shoot right up into the air, as though released like a rocket from a ramp below. Again and again the men in the boat attempted to make progress towards the landing, with the man in the bows looking out for the cliffs through the spray. Every now and again he shouted 'left!' or 'right!', and the rower exerted all his muscular power to heave the boat in the right direction. When the sea rose and fell against the wall of the cliff, the boat went into reverse and then, as the water sucked back, it was steered towards the minute strip of beach with fast zigzagging strokes of the oars.

This manœuvring went on for a long time before we finally gave up. The seas were quite impossible that day and we had no alternative but to turn back. The windy weather continued for a couple of days. Camilla and I wandered around with the tape-recorder and parabolic reflector. In a small valley behind the hotel, protected from the wind, we recorded various bird sounds. We also spent some time meandering along the small beaches, enjoying the idyllic surroundings in the sun and wind. However hard the wind blew it was never chilly.

When we were planning the next attempt to get to St Giles, I asked Mr Lau to arrange for us to start immediately before dawn. I had noticed that the wind was noticeably less in the early hours of the day. We were able to get out through the fringe of sharp rocks just as first light was breaking. The swell was somewhat less than on the previous occasion and I thought to myself that this time our luck would hold.

Each camera was sealed in plastic bags before being put into the kitbags which, in turn, were wrapped up in plastic sheets. The equipment was bulky and included various valuables: tape-recorder, all the cameras, parabolic reflector and the rest of the equipment, plus water-bottles and a load of fruit. There was too much to take over in one go, and we reckoned that three trips would be necessary assuming the first landing was successful.

It was. When we finally reached the small fringe of rippling coral sand, I seized a couple of the kitbags and jumped ashore together with the look-out man. The next wave came rushing in but we were already beyond its reach with our loads. The man at the oars worked like mad to get out through the barrier of rocks. He went back for another load and returned with the remainder of the equipment. All went well and after a third trip the water and food were safely landed.

I was given help with the packages up the cliff, which was covered by a hanging mat of green vegetation. It was like climbing up a big net which sometimes came adrift from the cliff face. About 150 feet up there was a clump of trees. We paused here to get our breath back, leaning the kitbags on the steep slope against the trees. The thunderous roar from the waves below almost drowned the screams from the boobies and terns flying around us. From this height the waves seemed enormous and the boat no larger than a toy one.

One of the boys borrowed my bush-knife and, grinning broadly, cut himself a stick six feet long. I thought he wanted this to help him down the slope, but to my astonishment and exasperation he made a quick swipe with it and hit a young red-footed booby on the nape while it was in its nest on a branch. Still grinning he grabbed it and sprang down the green net ladder towards the boat, which then chugged away. We had arranged that it should return in five days' time, wind permitting, to take me off the island. Five days of solitary existence awaited me but whereas Robinson Crusoe had the charming island of Tobago for companion, I was surrounded by cliffs with bearded cacti glaring at me from all sides.

I had been landed at the weakest point of the rock fortress, and the vegetation would have provided a completely impenetrable barrier if I had not had my bush-knife with me. Cutting a way through the rain-forest involves constantly looking up to avoid the many bees' and ants' nests. In the thicket of cactus plants I had to contend with cactus stems powerfully armed with sharp spines.

Cacti are elegant plants and in some ways it seemed quite irresponsible to be hacking at these big clumps. A quick oblique blow, and the whole of the long spike slides down on its cut surface, bounces lightly on the ground and topples over, lying as rigid as a pole. This was easy compared with the terrible labour of cutting through the black, springy and extremely hard wood of the scrub, which formed small but dense belts. After a couple of hours it became unbearably hot and the sweat seemed to raise my temperature instead of cooling down the body. As the sun beat vertically down I had to ruffle my shock of hair and shield my eyes from the glare with one hand. I felt quite dizzy and there is always the risk of sunstroke in these parts. It was much too hot to have worn a hat.

I eventually came to a dead tree and climbed up it. I was rewarded with a view over almost the whole of the island. At the other end of the cactus thicket, still some distance away, I could see a cloud of birds surging in the sky. This was where I was aiming for because the frigate-birds were nesting in that part of the island. I knew that they were not shy at the nest and that their fascinating pair formation ceremonies would be particularly suitable for filming. During the breeding season the male frigate-bird has a large red throat sac which he inflates like a balloon. With this gaudy adornment he tries to attract a female who hovers over him motionlessly on wings of six-foot span. I had seen an American film of the courtship behaviour of *Fregata minor*, which nests amongst other places in parts of the Galapagos Islands, and I wanted to film the corresponding behaviour in *Fregata magnificens*, the rather larger species found on St Giles.

I continued my way through the thicket of scrub but the muscles in my arms began to ache and it was with some relief that I came to a large area of long grass. Here I had only to push my way through. More cactus and belts of scrub followed but I had the feeling that I would soon reach the edge of a precipice, from where I could take some wide-angle shots of the bird cliffs in the distance. I had not realised how long it would take to clear a path or else I would have brought some food with me. Having suffered from diabetes since childhood, I have to be careful to balance the amount of insulin with the intake of carbohydrate. Going without food in my case can be dangerous. As a result of my strenuous exertions, I suddenly realised I was suffering from insulin shock. I knew that this meant that the amount of sugar—the energy source—in the blood was dwindling and that I must get back quickly.

The belt of grass, through which I had earlier forced my way quite easily, presented me with a problem on the return route. The grass had straightened up again and there was no sign of any track. I had not taken a compass with me for this short trip, and the sun was so high that it gave me no help in finding my direction. I lost my way and began to feel the insulin shock all the more.

When I got back to the scrub belt again, I started to cut through it with feeble strokes; my muscles began to quiver and my heart felt heavy as lead, due to lack of the necessary 'fuel.' At all costs I had to get back to where I had left the food. I forced my way on through the cacti, not having sufficient strength to cut a path. I soon realised I was completely lost. The wind was constant and I tried to remember from which direction it had come when I was sitting up in the dead tree at the beginning of the trip; I tried to work out a direction and staggered on. I was lacerated by thorns; cactus spines had lodged in my feet, legs, hands, and arms, but I scarcely felt them. I knew that time was running out and that if I did not get back quickly it was very doubtful if I would ever do so. I had fits of dizziness in the heat and the insulin shock was worse than any that I had ever experienced. It slowed down my mental processes to such an extent that I was acting more or less like a sleep-walker. When I finally found some bushes which had already been cut I was shaking like a jelly and swayed along the path marked by mutilated cacti. At last I recognised the sounds of the sea mixed with the calls of boobies and sooty terns.

'Food, glorious food!' A phrase from the song came into my mind and with Oliver Twist's notes ringing in my head, I stuffed biscuits into my mouth with trembling hands. The sheer pleasure of eating in such a situation is beyond description; it has to be experienced to be believed.

I spent the whole of the rest of that day and the next cutting paths. While I was working I was watched by a large flock of birds flying above me. The frigate-birds, looking like hundreds of crosses hanging motionless in the sky, kept watch on me without uttering a sound and making no sign of movement in the strong breeze. Only now and again one dropped quickly back in its characteristic way, changing places with another in the uniform pattern of stations held by the flock. I built my photographic hide on a protruding section of cliff with a view over some nests of terns and boobies. Boobies live up to their name and their apparent lack of fear often results in their death at the hands of man.

Hurricane Flora had left its mark even on St Giles. According to Mr Lau, the whole island, which had previously shone with white dots, representing birds, was swept completely clean. Although the birds had returned, the boobies seemed to be low in numbers when I was there.

The hide was perched on a loose heap of stones on the edge of a precipice with a 150-foot drop to the powerful breakers below. I tied a rope round my leg and attached the other end to a tree trunk. Although the hide was constructed of loose branches it quickly became unbearably hot inside. The young boobies hung untidily half out of the nest as though they were dead, their necks pointing towards the shark-infested waters below. After some hours I saw one actually fall out. I did not see how it came about but I caught sight of a fluttering white body plummeting below me.

There were some nests near by of the noddy tern, a brownish-black tern with a pale spot on the forehead. The name comes from the greeting ceremony performed when two of them meet: they lower their heads towards each other as though they were bowing, almost Japanese style. In general one should guard against interpreting the actions of animals according to human patterns, but in this case it is justified. By exposing its most vulnerable spot the tern indicates its lack of hostility towards its partner or neighbour. A quick blow with a sharp beak aimed at the nape and the tern would be dead. This gesture therefore has a disarming effect in a critical situation. The male wolf makes a similar gesture of submission when it acknowledges defeat by a more powerful male. In man greetings are based on the same fundamental motivation. We take off our hats and bow, bending the head forward into a more vulnerable position. We extend a hand, originally to demonstrate that there is no weapon in it. The head-bowing display has a disarming effect only within the species. When a sooty tern comes too near to a noddy tern the former spreads out a wing, making itself appear as large as possible, but even so receives a strong peck on its open beak.

I continued to cut paths, slowly but surely, surrounded by terns and increasing hordes of frigate-birds, or man-o'-war birds. I could not help wondering whether their inquisitiveness was not responsible for their name. If some privateer lay in the lee of an island where frigate-birds were nesting, other sailors should have been able to spot it from the midge-like swarm of birds with six-foot wing-spans marking it from above.

I kept making steady progress through the dense mat of cactus which separated the two halves of St Giles. In this area the cacti grew so densely that when I had hacked them off I had to remove them and stack them in heaps. By this time my whole body ached from the inflammation of the pricks I had received; small detached awls decorated most areas of my body and it was difficult to find a clear patch of skin for my daily insulin injection.

As I was cutting my route I suddenly noticed that another path had crossed mine. The marks of the cuts were old and the new cacti were growing up among the decapitated pillars. I began to follow this winding path although sometimes it was difficult to see which way it went. To my surprise every now and again I came across considerable piles of feathers. Then I noticed the wing of a bird, and saw that it had been cut off. I found more of these remains and came to the conclusion that the path had been made by people who had leapt ashore on to some ledge far below and then plundered the booby nests.

I reckoned that in a few hours I would be able to get over to the part of the island where the frigate-birds lived. I could see the nesting area through my binoculars and it was white with down. In spite of this I decided to go no farther. I felt I had already done sufficient damage. Although the island is privately owned and should be free of trespassers and nest robbers, I knew very well the respect with which such prohibitions were treated in these parts. My path, broad and fine, could serve as a basic route for bird thieves from Tobago. I decided not to risk extending it all the way to the area where the best colonies were.

I sat on one of the look-out points at dusk and looked out over the island covered with cacti. The setting sun was surrounded by thin red veils of cloud which were shrouded in hazy mist. Huge flocks of the magnificent frigate-birds moved in towards the half of the island which was guarded by cacti; it was as though the whole of the reddening sky was full of these living crosses.

I had lost the battle for the fortress, the inhabitants were safe behind their palisades of long pin-cushions. I hoped that they would long remain so.

# 9 *Flamingo island*

Lying approximately on the same latitude as Trinidad and Tobago but about five hundred miles farther west there are three Dutch islands whose names start with the first letters of the alphabet. They are Aruba, Bonaire and Curaçao. The last is well known for its liqueur, which is pronounced curaçao or corrosao on the island, depending on whether the speaker uses Dutch, English or papiamento. Papiamento is a mixed language, much the same as the patois spoken in Trinidad, particularly up in the mountain districts, but with Dutch, Spanish and Indian dialects as the principal ingredients. In contrast to the position in Trinidad, this mixed language is regarded here as a proper language, and the radio news bulletins are also given in a papiamento version.

After my stay on St Giles I would have preferred to go to a place where there were no cacti at all, but on Curaçao and Bonaire I definitely fell out of the frying-pan into the fire. These islands might be described as the Promised Land for cacti. Gigantic branched specimens compete with small creeping relatives of a most peculiar appearance. Bonaire, where I was constantly on the move, was a forest of needles. Although the shops stocked everything from French scent to underwater cameras and jewellery, there was surprisingly not a single pair of boots for sale.

To get to Bonaire, which was my real goal, one has first to go to Curaçao, which is the administrative and commercial centre for the islands. Its proximity to Maracaibo, the oil distribution centre for Venezuela, has given Curaçao a key position with its notable harbour in the capital at Willemstad. Tankers and bunkering ships of all kinds call here, and on the basis of the total tonnage passing through it is reckoned as number four in the harbours of the world. The customs policy in Curaçao is one of the reasons for its popularity as a tourist centre. Tourists can buy cameras, watches and jewels remarkably cheaply without paying import duty, which is only 3 % for the island's resident population.

The Caribbean Marine Biological Institute lies a short distance from Willemstad. Before leaving Sweden I had been given a lot of good advice and contacts by Bengt Sjögren, whose book *Islands around the Wind* had strongly influenced my choice of the West Indian islands as a place to work in. He had advised me to get in touch with Dr I. Kristensen, Director of the Marine Biological Institute, for information about the flamingoes in which I was particularly interested. However, I found that Dr Kristensen was away on an expedition and instead I got in touch with Dr F. Creuzberg, who was in charge of the Institute in his absence.

Together with Dr Creuzberg and his family, Camilla and I drove out to a small lagoon where formerly salt was worked in large shallow pools. The labour was provided from a prison situated on one of the shores. In the centre of this salty lagoon lies a very small island. When I was in Willemstad I went into one of the well-stocked bookshops and by chance happened to glance at a book about birds. I found there a picture and a brief reference in the text to a report that some years ago about a thousand Cayenne terns had turned up in Curaçao and had chosen the little island in the salt lagoon as a nesting place. Since then the tern colony has grown considerably, and I believe that the population now numbers between three and four thousand birds.

When we approached the island it appeared to be densely populated with nesting terns, spaced out so that neighbouring pairs were just out of reach of each other's bills. The colony looked like a snowfield spreading all over the island. Every now and again there was a ripple of movement in the colony and the birds would rise into the air like a flurry of snowflakes and then settle down again in their respective places. The contrast of a snowstorm in the heat of the dry salt landscape was most striking.

The following day Dr Creuzberg and I returned to the salt lake. I took cameras and tape-recorder with me as well as a baby's plastic bath. I placed the cameras in the bath and swam out to the terns, pushing the small craft ahead of me. The water was repulsively salty, but I was able to float like a cork and had no difficulty in balancing the plastic ship with its valuable cargo. The terns showed no sign of alarm and allowed me to stay among them, apparently accepting my presence without any marked reaction. Though they flew up every now and again, I had already seen them doing this in the distance the day before and I am almost sure that this is normal behaviour, perhaps to cool the eggs, the young and themselves.

The big colony gave the impression of being a well-drilled army or a gigantic, attentive audience. All the birds were facing in the same direction, heads pointing straight into the wind, which is a common phenomenon among birds resting in regions where strong winds blow continuously. Like aeroplanes they have to take off into the wind. When a small flock of terns flew up from their eggs, they remained in the air for a time, wings flapping in the breeze, and then all sank down to land on their nests and exchange a few quick thrusts with their yellow bills, which serve as measuring rods. The younger birds show a certain amount of grey on the bill.

Having landed the cameras safely I swam back, loaded up the tape-recorder, and swam out to the island again. As I finished my recordings I heard some loud toots coming from the shore. Dr Creuzberg had driven me out in the Institute's Volkswagen bus and I assumed that the signals implied that he wanted to get back, so I began to gather up my tapes and cables. Although I waved to him the tooting went on and I soon discovered why.

The bath-tub which I had anchored with a large stone had nevertheless capsized in the wind and floated away. It was already a couple of hundred yards off. I swam as fast as I could and caught up with it after a chase of half a mile. I turned the craft round and started to swim back but in this direction the wind was against me. After a time I was forced to give up, for the water was blown into my mouth and, worse still, my eyes. The smarting sensation was indescribable and the salinity so high that I was forced to turn towards the shore where the prison was.

The episode had a kind of inverted Count of Monte Cristo flavour. Edmond Dantes swam away from a prison but I swam towards one. When I actually landed my eyes were so sore that I was afraid I had damaged the cornea. I stood for a long time with my head down, letting the tears run and cleanse the eyeballs, until the smarting pain gradually eased. I then walked back round the edge of the lake with the plastic tub. I suffered no ill effects from my salty outing but I was soon sporting a tan of the reddest kind and the whites of my eyes were also rather red.

I was to see more of the salt lakes on Bonaire. There are two of these on the island. The one which lies in the centre is called Goto Lac and is surrounded by high, rocky beaches; the other, Pekelmeer, at the south-eastern tip of the island, is so shallow as to be intensely saline. At one time salt was extracted here by slave labour, and while we were there an American company was researching into the possibility of resuming salt production. If its results proved satisfactory this would bring some benefits to the small human population but at the same time would be dangerous, indeed probably fatal, to the flamingo colony on the island which was the main reason for my journey to Bonaire.

*Phoenicopterus ruber* deserves its specific name. It is the reddest of the six different kinds of flamingo found in the world. Like the scarlet ibis it is rapidly decreasing in numbers, but unlike the ibis, the destruction of flamingoes has received a lot of publicity and everything is being done to preserve the few sites that remein. At present the biggest nesting colony is said to be on Great Inagua, one of the Bahamas. This is a very large island and at its centre there is an extensive salt lake where the flamingoes build their nests on banks far removed from man. About six thousand birds are said to nest there. Elsewhere the species occurs on some other islands in the Caribbean Sea, on the Yucatan peninsula, in places along eastern South America down to the Falkland Islands, in Peru on the west coast and now and again on the Galapagos Islands, approximately six hundred miles from the coast of Ecuador.

It has been estimated that the total population of the species has fallen from around 90,000 to about 21,000. The greatest danger comes from modern methods of communication. Aeroplanes thundering in over the unprotected areas, which form the nesting habitat of the flamingoes, have repeatedly prevented the Bonaire colony from nesting. In 1943, as a result of U.S. military aircraft flying over the island, the birds all left and did not return until four years later, whereupon they nested again. Commercial aircraft now make a big detour past the southern end of the island, and Bonaire's own Flamingo Airport lies at a safe distance from Pekelmeer.

The flamingo has no 'natural' enemies on Bonaire and no one shoots them or steals the eggs or young, as happens elsewhere. The last time someone raided the flamingo chicks he was severely punished: two months in gaol. In this connection it is worth mentioning the punishment meted out to the poachers who damaged the ibis nesting in Trinidad: they were fined five pounds. Various other kinds of amusement cost no less than this, and with such a light punishment the guarding of a protected area becomes almost a matter for ridicule.

The list of animal species on Bonaire is very poor. The terrain is flat, sun-baked, and salt around Pekelmeer but the farther one goes in other directions the more fertile it becomes. There are forests of waving vegetation, unfortunately consisting only of branching cacti. There are also trees but these are rather sparse. One called *divi-divi* is unquestionably a handsome sight with the crowns turned at a sharp angle to one side, all pointing away from the wind. The wind is perpetually present, and one cannot escape it anywhere except in the lee of the rocky outcrops far to the west. In this area occurs a giant armada of minute winged insects, all too ready to bite savagely.

The cacti are popular with the Caribbean parrakeet, *Aratinga pertinax*. These elegant small birds with their yellow, green and blue plumage are an attractive feature in the prickly landscape. They eat the small cactus fruits with enthusiasm, moving in flocks through the thickets and uttering loud screams, the only sound that has a chance to carry for more than ten or twenty yards against the roar of the wind and the wash of the waves in the coral gravel.

Bonaire is a coral island consisting of piles of dead antler corals and brain corals on volcanic rock. The swishing of water on the pieces of coral seems to have infected the bird-song. The little yellow-and-grey sugar-bird or bananaquit, which sings an enchanting little descant in the rain-forests of Trinidad, has evolved on Bonaire into a subspecies. Its song is like a short echo of the sounds along the beach. The only sound that delights the ear is the short solo at twilight of the tropical mockingbird, whose varied phrases are a compromise between those of a song thrush and the more penetrating notes of a nightingale.

I was very pleased to find hummingbirds in this desert-dry landscape. Two species occur on Bonaire and I witnessed several fights between a small sugar-bird which was guarding an agave bloom, the only one within sight, and a brilliant little male ruby-topaz hummingbird. Its name ruby-topaz is well-deserved; the head of the male is a glossy red, the 'bib' is golden, and as the bird hovers these colours flash in glorious fashion.

Camilla and I stayed at the Flamingo Beach Club. The hotel is run by Don Stewart, an American who is interested in the brightly coloured species of fish which live on the coral-reef at depths of about 30 to 60 feet. Don couldn't understand why I spent my time filming on dry land when there was so much colourful life underwater. Unfortunately on my first visit I had left the underwater casing for

*A romantic moonlight scene—a pair of opossums courting.*

the camera behind and so had to accept his slightly acid comments.

In the Dutch handbook which I had studied, the nesting season for the flamingoes on the island was given as May and the following months. If I had paid more attention to Bengt Sjögren's book I would have obtained the correct information, which is that the peak of the nesting season is in February. It was May when I first visited Bonaire and all the flamingo chicks had been fully fledged for a long time. Grey and lanky, a couple of hundred were still wandering about in the nesting area, accompanied by some brilliant pink adults. When the chicks are able to fly well enough to undertake a long journey they set off for the mainland. The young flamingoes we saw walking about in the salt lake were the last of the year to leave. However, as we were being driven along the road to Pekelmeer, Mr Ellis, of Bonaire's tourist office, told us that he had recently seen at least a thousand flamingoes on the beach.

Every assistance was given to our plans to reach them. A car was put at our disposal at the island's expense for a couple of days and we undertook a reconnaissance. The tourist office also arranged for me to receive the help of Mr Mayer, who, apart from his car-hire activities, does a lot of photography, mainly with the flamingo as his subject. He confirmed that it would not be possible at this stage of the season to get close to the birds without making them take off.

It was annoying to be faced with the prospect of having nothing at all to film, but I decided to make an attempt the following day. Camilla and I drove out to Pekelmeer where we found a small flock still present. The water shone pink, bright pink, a colour caused by the mass occurrence of the very small brine shrimp, *Artemia salina*. The adult flamingoes looked as though they were reflections from this water, but of a darker shade.

ABOVE *I used the underwater casing for my film camera when I swam with the anaconda in fresh water and also in the salt water of Bonaire's colourful coral-reef.* BELOW *The water at Bonaire is extraordinarily clear and the swarms of organisms at depths of 30 to 60 feet are a great attraction to a cameraman.*

I was unable to use any camouflage. I thought that instead it might be possible to practise a little deception, as birds base their reactions on a less complex set of associations than man. On early spring nights in Sweden I have been able to get eagle owls to start their evening concert by calling to them while squatting owl-fashion and flapping my arms at intervals. I hop about from rock to rock, waving my arms like fluttering wing-beats and before starting to make my call I display a white handkerchief under my chin. This sounds silly and must look daft, but the owls react to it on a really dark night, when even their light-sensitive retina has its limitations.

As my approach to the flamingoes was made with the sun setting behind me I reckoned that they would not see me very clearly. I fixed the camera to the tripod, fitted it with a medium-sized lens and began to walk out on the pink bottom of the lake. This consisted almost entirely of particles of salt and made a crunching noise as I waded. There were still places apparently where the birds could find something to eat; the micro-organisms on which they live have a fantastic resistance to salt and also to high concentrations of other substances which would be lethal to most animals.

I had more than half a mile to wade, so there was plenty of time to practise my role. What a performance it was! I held the tripod above my head like a flamingo neck, the lens representing the bill, and began to walk towards the birds. I had every chance to study the gait of flamingoes and imitate their style as the flock was right ahead of me. I followed a zigzag course, slowly reducing the distance between me and the birds. Now and again I lowered the tripod towards the surface of the water, making sweeping movements as though I were feeding.

As I got nearer some of the flamingoes raised their heads and gazed towards me for a time, making goose-like cackling calls. I quickly acquired this dialect and cackled out some replies, whereupon the company went back to immersing their heads in the pink soup. I got within 30 or 40 yards before beginning to film. I cackled at intervals and received preoccupied answers. We talked in this fashion of the weather and the wind, a safe subject. I also got an answer from a small flock which moved in from the east, looking like long sticks with pairs of wings beating in the middle. We exchanged a few friendly phrases and the whole company landed only about ten yards from me. They stared a little mistrustfully at the unusually thick-legged flamingo silhouette and then moved off towards the rest of the flock.

I was then able to study their food searching movements at rather closer range. The shape of the bill in any species of bird varies according to the way in which it is used. A bird of prey has a sharp, curved beak adapted for tearing its prey apart, a woodpecker has a powerful hammer-like tool, and a hawfinch has a pair of nutcrackers. The sword-billed hummingbird, *Ensifera*, has a bill that is longer than its body; it is so long that the bird has to feed the young while hovering on whirring wings, but it is perfectly adapted for feeding from the long flower-heads found in its normal surroundings.

The flamingo's remarkable bill and its whole make-up are also adapted for life in its own particular set of environmental conditions, including that of feeding on small organisms in salt lakes. It is particularly well adapted to surroundings in which large amounts of food are spread out in a thin layer at the bottom of the water. The long legs and neck can work together in depths of more than 18 inches. The feet stir up the bottom layer and the bill is passed back and forth like a vacuum-cleaner. The lower half of the bill is thicker than the upper, in contrast to the usual arrangement of the bill in other species, and it is also sharply angled. The inside of the bill is partially covered with hair-like lamellae, and with fast movements—three to four per second—the big muscular tongue presses the incoming food against them and produces food masses which are swallowed at regular intervals.

From time to time I saw some of the flamingoes 'cycling.' As the bird suddenly hops up and down, leaving its head concealed in the water, it looks as though it is pedalling a bicycle. This action probably stirs up the bottom, so that even large items of food such as small snails are disturbed from among the small particles of salt. The bottom is uncommonly rich in food in spite of its salinity or, more correctly, on account of it. Crustaceans, algae and fly larvae must be produced in enormous quantities to feed as many as three thousand flamingoes, each one measuring about four feet.

By this time my socks and gym shoes were soaking wet and it was time to turn back. As I withdrew I adopted the movements prescribed by my role: stepping elegantly, cackling, and waving the camera and tripod like a long neck. None of the birds was disturbed and I soon reached the shore. Camilla had watched all this through field glasses and laughed so much that I nearly had to give her artificial respiration. After this episode I devoted myself to the other animals on the island, mostly lizards and birds, and occasionally watched the flamingoes, which became fewer and fewer. One day I saw a flock moving away out over the sea towards Venezuela. Instead of turning in to land, as previously, the birds continued on a dead straight course until I lost sight of them.

It was time for us to travel back to Trinidad, but I made up my mind to return some time to see the flamingo colony during the peak of the breeding when numbers would be really high.

As my expedition was later extended to cover a whole year, a return trip to Bonaire became possible during the following breeding season. I remembered Don Stewart's teasing remarks about filming on land instead of underwater and on this trip I brought with me the underwater casing for my film camera.

Our first visit to the flamingo island had taken place when the tourists were thinning out but our second visit coincided with the height of the tourist season. It is only a question of time before Bonaire is swamped by tourists. A big new hotel had been put up

*The bromelias provide a very important source of food for the hummingbirds. The species of hummingbird shown here,* Glaucis hirsuta, *belongs to a genus which is not particularly colourful. They live so hidden away in the rain-forests that they are usually called hermits.*

and served as an additional threat to the flamingoes. These are a great attraction and extraordinarily easy to approach. There is a convenient road running round Pekelmeer from which the birds can be seen at comparatively close quarters. It would be much better if passengers were forbidden to get out of their cars, as is the case at Hornborg Lake in Sweden when thousands of cranes are nesting there.

I witnessed a perfect example of disturbance to the colony one day when I was sitting in my hide. Having placed this in a bush on the previous day I was waiting for the large flock of birds to make their way into the shallow water off the shore. The water was quite deep at this season and its pink colour, which had been so striking during May, was now much less noticeable. The rainy season had just ended and the teeming masses of micro-organisms provided plenty of food for the big flocks. The steel-grey sea made a fine contrast with the pink and red birds, and when a cloud swept over the sun the visual effect was most striking. The colours reflected from below were a deep red, gradually becoming pinker as the cloud thinned out again.

A flock of about a thousand flamingoes was assembling just beyond the hide when I suddenly saw a wave of movement pass through them. Their heads had been down and with necks visible among the crowd of legs the size of the flock seemed larger by fifty per cent. Then their necks went up just as though a wave had washed

ABOVE Colibri serrirostris *demonstrates the flying technique of the hummingbirds, which is unique in the bird world. In the wing or arm skeleton only the shoulder-joint is movable; the wing-beat frequency is constant, in one species about 80 wing-beats per second, and according to the position of the shoulder-joint the bird can remain stationary in the air, reverse, or fly forwards. Over a quarter of the body weight is represented by flight muscle, and in certain species the daily requirement of nectar is more than seven times the body weight.* BELOW *Two quite newly hatched hummingbird chicks of the species* Chrysolampis mosquitus. *Compare their size with that of an ordinary wedding-ring. My ring encircles them in the nest and is enlarged to twice its normal size in this picture.*

over them all. A car could be heard approaching and the hum of the engine blended with the notes of the cackling flamingoes. The car stopped, a door slammed, and high-pitched voices could be heard amongst the calls of the birds. Without undue commotion, the flock started to move out from the shore.

A man carrying a camera appeared in the foreground of the scene and bending down at the edge of the beach he picked up a lump of coral the size of a man's fist and chucked it out into the middle of the flock. One of the birds darted off, taking wing, and the whole of the rest of the flock followed suit. They made an exquisite picture and the man with the camera took snaps diligently. In a sense I should have been grateful to him because he had enabled me to take ciné pictures of the whole colony in flight. The man walked back to the car to be met by a stream of admiring comments. The car snarled into action and disappeared in a cloud of dust.

An example of a more serious kind of disturbance came to my notice the day after I arrived. To my delight I had already seen from the road, with the aid of binoculars, two groups of birds nesting on the far side of the lake. I had reported this to Mr Mayer, who acted as my guide on the previous visit. Later in the hotel, however, a pleasant couple had come up to me and chatted about this and that. They knew I had come to film the flamingoes, and to my dismay one of them said:

'You should have been with us this morning when we flew here. A wonderful sight! It would have been marvellous on TV, thousands of red birds flying below us. It was absolutely superb!'

They had hired a plane in Curaçao and flown out for a short excursion. They had happened to choose Bonaire as a suitable place for a bite of food and a bathe in the sea. As I have already mentioned, flying low over a colony presents the greatest possible threat to the flamingoes. In the nesting season they are particularly susceptible to disturbance.

Alarmed by this news I passed on the information to Mr Mayer and we walked over to the colony early next morning. As the sun warmed our backs, casting long shadows at our feet, Mr Mayer related sundry episodes from the birds' history on the island. He mentioned that in 1939, just before the outbreak of war, the number of birds in the colony had been estimated at over 10,000. Numbers had since declined and last year it was estimated that 3,000 had nested.

Our shadows shortened and ahead of us we saw a long pale pink band on the horizon. The pink glow became stronger and revealed itself as the nesting colony of the flamingoes. We continued on up to a grassy slope which was three or four hundred yards from the birds. Before long the birds folded their long legs and with necks swaying from side to side settled down one after the other. Their nests were about eight inches high and we were thankful to see that the birds had not left them. There were perhaps five to six hundred birds in this group, all settled on their nests.

Through the glasses we could see a number of eggs, perhaps three hundred, in another group, but here a catastrophe had taken place. There was not a single bird incubating them. Two days previously I had seen two groups of birds incubating. Since the aircraft's flight over the colony one group had deserted their eggs. Mr Mayer was relieved to see that at least the larger group of birds was still there. He told me that people from both Dutch and German TV were expected here soon and he was to act as guide for them. He described how previous groups of television people had gone straight out to the nesting site as the young began to hatch, and filmed the chicks gathered into groups and the parents flying off in a large flock.

Earlier I had seen Mr Mayer's own photographs. One of them showed two groups of newly hatched young and a large number of eggs in the mud nests, together with a cloud of red birds in the air. It made an attractive colour picture, but the enormous disturbance involved in obtaining it made it seem gruesome. My sole aim was to film the birds at a distance, showing them quietly incubating their eggs. I was also keen to film them later feeding the young.

While we sat in front of the flamingo colony I was able to film the birds at the nest as they quietly adjusted their positions, standing up in their typically unsteady manner and then sitting right down again. In the morning sun they glowed a beautiful salmon-pink. When I had filmed the birds incubating, Mr Mayer stood up, which made the whole colony unfold their long legs like a battalion on parade. As we left I could not help feeling concerned about the disturbance which would obviously result from future guided tours for television.

During the following two weeks I followed Don Stewart's advice and went under water to see Bonaire from its most enchanting angle. Thirty-one species of shark are found around the coasts of the islands but during all my underwater excursions I did not see a single specimen. I wasn't sorry since I never hunt under water and therefore never take a harpoon with me. Don had no time to dive before the afternoon, which is when the sharks are most dangerous, according to an American investigation on the frequency of shark attacks. No shark appeared, and everything was peaceful and the scenery exquisite, both in colour and form.

Don never dived without his little fish-net, a small perforated container for the fish that he caught, and also his secret mixture, a solution which attracted certain fish species and which he squirted in small doses into the cavities in the coral-reef. We mostly stayed at depths between 30 and 60 feet. In this zone we had marvellous views of brain corals as large as a dinner table, cup-sponges like wine butts, and waving sea-fans. We were surrounded by small fish, large fish, vertical, horizontal, four-cornered and disc-shaped fishes in all the shapes and sizes that a human brain could imagine. The activities of the shoals, with their sharply contrasting colours and markings, provided a constantly changing visual pattern which in some ways was akin to the varied acoustic pattern heard in the chorus of bird-song on a spring morning in the north. The silence under the sea helps perhaps to emphasise the effect of colour.

As one floats in the blue underwater world, gliding along without exertion and far removed from reality, one's whole body is pervaded with a sense of well-being. This sensation is in itself a danger. If one dives too deep, the feeling that everything is perfect grows and one is convinced of one's omnipotence. It has happened that people intoxicated by the depths have torn off their compressed air equipment for the pure joy of living—and thus suddenly put an end to life itself.

The water in these parts is almost unbelievably transparent. Wearing a snorkel and floating on the surface like a mosquito larva, one looks down at the panorama below to select a section to examine in detail, and the bottom appears very close, perhaps only fifteen feet away. As one exchanges the snorkel for the mouthpiece of the full diving equipment, brain corals the size of a football gradually assume the dimensions of a sunshade and the depth gauge registers some sixty feet.

On this peaceful reef there was a great variety of marine life. Only sharks were absent. Small shy cuttlefish blushed like schoolgirls and withdrew discreetly downwards; gigantic lobsters with antennae like fishing-rods sat in meditation and parrotfish glided forward with teeth like large pincers; marine angelfish in yellow and black played awkwardly with butterflyfish while trumpetfish glided in their vertical hunting position over small groups of unsuspicious squirrelfish. Small boxfish, all encased in bone, stared me in the face and a shoal of triggerfish moved up and down like a curtain. The feeling of freedom as one glides around in the clear warm water over a 3,000-foot precipice gives one the impression more of flying than of swimming, like a human buzzard soaring close to the edge of a mountain.

The shoals of differently coloured fishes, with their various shades of blue, made a great visual impression on me and I could still see them in my mind as I waited on the shore of the Pekelmeer, with its vast wealth of food, to take close-ups of the pink flamingoes. On the advice of Mr Mayer I had gone out to the nesting area a little later on to see how the birds were progressing with their incubation and whether any chicks had hatched. I had not been very happy about the rather abrupt method of approaching the colony adopted on the previous occasion. I decided to use quite a different technique this time.

I set out before dawn. The salt company had placed a straight line of sticks right between the two halves of the colony. I counted the sticks as I walked along in the dark, and when there were only two left between me and the spot where Mr Mayer and I had sat down on the bank, I started to crawl forward on my hands and knees. The ground was covered by a stone-like salt crust, and I had attached pads of foam plastic under my pullover and trouser knees. After crawling for a time I reached the grassy bank and set up the film camera, waiting for the light to come.

The birds had not noticed me at all. Lying on my stomach I was able to film life going on peacefully in the colony. I personally enjoyed this far more than all the magnificence of red-winged birds frightened into flight, promised by Mr Mayer. Now and again some of the birds got up and beat their wings powerfully for a short time, then stretched their long necks down, rolled the egg into the saucer of the nest and sank down over their treasured possession, rocking backwards and forwards a little to get the egg in position before settling down to incubate.

To my delight I also saw some greyish-white balls of down among the long red legs on the outskirts of the colony. Some of the flamingo chicks had already hatched. After a while flamingoes began to fly in over the pink area, coming singly or in small groups, either to change over at the nest for a spell of incubation or just to greet their mates.

After my long watch in a cramped position I felt decidedly stiff, but I crawled away until I was sufficiently far off to risk walking in a crouched position. Even when I adopted this gait, the birds took no more notice of me than if I had been one of the goats which often wander about in the neighbourhood of the colony. Hence my belief that one should take time and trouble over the best way to approach animals, whether they are flamingoes or any other species.

The colony I had been filming probably included all the birds actually breeding at that time. The low-flying aircraft had not only frightened away a section of the colony, it had also broken the chain reaction which is part of the nesting process of colonial species. The section of the colony which had been frightened away and had left for good was the one which had started egg-laying latest. It might have been followed by one or even two more groups.

When we returned to Curaçao I discussed the partially unsuccessful breeding with Dr Creuzberg. He told me of an additional factor which caused serious disturbance to the flamingoes—smugglers. The customs policy in Curaçao and the other Dutch islands is favourable to smugglers, for in nearby Venezuela there is a high rate of customs duty. Creuzberg had woken up in the night on one occasion and seen for himself stacks of boxes being loaded quite openly on to a boat from the landing-stage of the Institute.

Smuggling by air is also common, with aeroplanes flying low at night. If a plane travels over Bonaire's flamingo colony at night this finishes the nesting for that year. Even if every pilot is warned about the prohibition of flying over certain areas it will always be impossible to exercise complete control over these illegal night flights.

# 10 *Flying jewels*

The large flocks of pink and red flamingoes on Bonaire and the flocks of deep scarlet ibis in Trinidad are natural phenomena of captivating beauty. The visual impression is one overflowing with colour but there is another group of birds which can still outshine them. Although they do not measure up to the mass effect of a panorama of flamingoes or ibises they represent nature's most finely drawn miniatures, in which brilliant patches of colour are positioned so that the effect of contrast is multiplied.

Most representatives of the family Trochilidae, the humming-birds, so sparkle with colour that it is not surprising that both their Latin and English names refer to jewels and glittering objects. The Latin name of the ruby-topaz hummingbird which I saw on Bonaire is *Chrysolampis mosquitus*, that is to say, 'the golden torch of mosquito build'. Other specific names have even more dazzling comparisons with such things as emerald, sapphire, turquoise, amethyst, tour-maline, diamond, gold, copper, bronze, the sun and stars—altogether a commendable but incomplete attempt to describe the brilliant ap-pearance of these small birds.

The family is confined to the New World. There are about 320 species altogether, of which 247 are found in South America. In the

*The humidity in the warm rain-forests is collected in streams and rivers, and all kinds of life thrive in this hot-house atmosphere. The tree in the foreground is decked with epiphytes, which only use the tree for support and are not parasitic.*

Old World there is a large gap and an evolutionary niche seems for once to have remained unoccupied. It is true that there are several species there which exploit the blooms, reaping a rich harvest in return for pollinating the flowers, but unlike the hummingbirds with their perfect flying and pumping techniques they are not so highly adapted for feeding on nectar.

When one sees a hummingbird in flight the astonishing feature is the speed and accuracy with which it changes its hovering position. Even if the wind is blowing hard, the little pump stands motionless in the billowing sea of air and refuels itself from a flower. The little craft moves off elegantly in reverse and with a fast forward flight arrives at the next source of energy. It is precisely this 'reverse gear' which is the special feature of the hummingbird. Within the world of birds its helicopter flight is unsurpassed, but insects and the nectar-sucking bats have the same or a similar patent.

To 'tread water' in this manner demands high frequency wing-beats, and at least among the smallest species these are incredibly fast. So far the highest known frequency occurs in the male of the Brazilian species, *Calliphlox amethystina*, with 80 wing-beats per second. This is not the smallest species in the family but nevertheless a lilliputian one with its body-weight of two grams. The giant among the hummingbirds is *Patagona gigas*, which lives in the Andes and is sometimes found at a height of 14,000 feet above sea level. It has a body-weight of about twenty grams and the lowest wing-beat frequency among hummingbirds, 8 to 10 per second.

A hummingbird darting forward appears to go like lightning, and measurements made from a car have shown a top speed of 60 mph in certain species. This method of measurement is not perhaps the most

*The leatherback turtle, the largest turtle in the world, may weigh over 1,200 pounds. It is very rare and high time the species was protected; otherwise it will soon become extinct on account of the senseless slaughter which takes place when the females come ashore to lay their eggs.*

reliable. Crawford H. Greenewalt, author of the excellent book *Hummingbirds*, tested the speed of certain species in a specially built wind-tunnel; he reported a maximum speed of about 27 mph, which is not much to boast of in the bird world. A helicopter, the machine which comes closest to nature's equivalent, is not a particularly fast form of aircraft, and it is amusing that measurements of the requirements per hour and per unit of weight for a highly tuned helicopter are shown to be almost the same as those for a hummingbird.

A hummingbird requires large quantities of fuel. Detailed investigations undertaken with certain species in glass containers in the laboratory, where oxygen consumption was measured under different conditions, have shown that its metabolism, as might be expected, is faster than in any other living creature. Per gram of body-weight, it is over a hundred times faster than in the elephant. The little bird has to whir all round its territory throughout the entire working day in order to fill up with fuel at the various blooms. It does this continuously apart from an hour's rest, which occurs at the same time every day, roughly between 11 am and 2 pm. This hour is used for sunbathing and singing.

The resemblance between a nectar-sucking hummingbird and a hypodermic syringe is striking and in the West Indies these birds also go under the name of 'doctor bird.' The burden of work on this small representative of the profession is heavy, and the 'doctor' has to dip into many flowers in order to keep its machinery in working order. Augusto Ruschi, the well-known expert on hummingbirds, weighed a frilled coquette, *Lophornis magnifica*, before and after a meal. There was an increase from 1.8 grams to 2.3 grams. It had therefore consumed more than a quarter of its own weight. During one day this little machine takes at least 17 grams of nectar or sugar solution, that is, over nine times its own weight in fuel. In addition it also eats insects, which satisfy its protein requirements.

These small birds are completely adapted for the effective exploitation of nectar. The tongue is long and tubular and serves as a suction tube which can be extended far beyond the lengthy bill.

Indeed, as I have already mentioned, there is one species, *Ensifera ensifera*, in which the bill is longer than the body. In the male of at least one species, *Pygmornis ruber*, the tongue is also used in a special display. During courtship the male hangs his tongue out like a pennant, which presumably the lady of his choice finds enchanting.

The perpetual pumping is intensified during the period before dusk. During the night the birds cannot fill up with fuel, a factor which gives an animal with a fast rate of metabolism a major problem. A pigmy shrew, with a metabolic rate approaching that of a hummingbird, must feed day and night in order not to die of starvation. The hummingbirds have solved the problem in the only way possible for them: by stalling the whole organism and saving their energy. When sleeping they go into a state of torpidity, their body temperature sinks to that of the surrounding air and, most important of all, the rate of metabolism is reduced to a fifteenth of what it is by day. The birds become as stiff as a piece of wood and they can be taken from their night perch without showing any sign of movement. Complete torpidity is not achieved until the bird's temperature has dropped by about seven degrees Centigrade, but it can then continue for as long as fourteen hours in certain regions of the far north or south where the winter nights are long.

Much remains to be found out about this interesting and varied family of birds. Their remarkable metabolic system can scarcely be fully assessed from studies made in the laboratory, though much has been done in America along these lines. If one looks at the results of such research, it would appear quite impossible for a ruby-throated hummingbird to cover more than 370 miles in a single flight. In fact it has been shown that this species flies in large flocks across the Gulf of Mexico, a distance of 500 miles at one stretch.

The most remarkable example of nature's handiwork in the field of vertebrates is supplied not by the adults but by their offspring. One cannot but marvel at the delicacy with which the young hummingbirds are built. In the picture of the nest of a ruby-topaz hummingbird two newly hatched chicks are seen within the compass of my wedding ring (19 millimetres internal diameter). Yet this species is a relatively large one. In the more lightly built *Lophornis magnifica*, each egg weighs only 0.3 gram and measures 12×8 millimetres.

In Trinidad I was able to film all three types of hummingbird nest. The commonest type is a small fine egg-cup placed so firmly on a branch that it lookes like a natural outgrowth or a broken-off twig. The second type of nest is a hanging structure, a cornet-shaped collection of thin roots and dry leaves, which is constructed under the fronds of ferns. Type number three is of quite different construction; it is made of such a coarse mesh that the eggs and young can be seen through the walls of the nest. The chicks are sometimes fed through the sides while the female remains motionless in the air outside and gives injections through the meshes in the airy cradle.

The real beauty in the hummingbird world, *Chrysolampis mosquitus*, which I saw on the desert-dry Bonaire, has been in danger of extinction. During the most turgid and macabre period of fashion in ladies' millinery, thousands of skins of this species were exported for the benefit of European women who lacked confidence in their own looks. It is hardly surprising that this species was so much in demand, since no other hummingbird has such extensive areas of iridescence in proportion to its body surface. The ruby-red on the head and the golden breast made the male one of the most striking among the jewels of the air.

The females of *Chrysolampis mosquitus* are much less flamboyant than the males, as in most species of hummingbird. In Trinidad I noticed to my joy that the ruby-topaz was anything but rare. In one area the size of an ordinary school yard, I saw seven nests of the species and filmed the feeding and development of the chicks in one of the nests. When the female arrived it looked as though the young were receiving advanced lessons in a school for sword-swallowers. Her whole bill went deep down into the gape of the young. It was almost as if she reached right down to the bottom of the nest with these injections. The chicks, which at first were not visible above the edge of the nest, gradually grew until they not only filled the nest but finally bulged over the side like fermenting yeast. Often the shape of the nest became completely deformed by the young, two in number as in all species of hummingbird.

I saw nests of six species of hummingbird in Trinidad, but the island which is often known as the land of hummingbirds actually has sixteen. This title would perhaps be more appropriate to Ecuador or possibly Colombia, the latter having 135 species. Among West Indian islands Trinidad leads the way, the others having seventeen species in all.

It is not surprising that hummingbirds thrive in Trinidad for the island is full of flowering vegetation. The immortelles cover the roof of the forests with a sea of orange blooms, rich in nectar, flowering over a long period. This coincides with the breeding periods of all the hummingbirds apart from the three species which are primarily insect-eaters. The flowering of the immortelles is followed by the yellow *poui*. This flowers in the middle of the dry season, making the forests look as though they were in autumn colours. The yellow colour disappears quickly because the flowering period is short, but the tree can light up like a suspended field of dandelions twice or sometimes three times a season. The related pink *poui* flowers only once a year and then overflows with amazing clouds of caramel pink blooms, also very popular with the hummingbirds.

An accusing finger can be pointed, by the way, at all male hummingbirds. Their whole life is spent in tippling nectar, fighting rivals, and running after mates. They never help with nest-building and incubation, nor with the care of the young, and their only task in life is to court females by the hour. This involves the display of all the patches of colour in their plumage, combined with purely acrobatic aerial displays according to the behaviour pattern of the species.

The songs of hummingbirds are comparatively nondescript, as is often the case in birds with very striking plumage. In one of the more drably coloured species which I was able to see and tape-record, a kind of music festival takes place in which a number of birds of the same species take part without any obvious signs of aggression. There appear to be communal singing arenas where ten or more individuals devote themselves to choir practice. I recorded this small brown species, *Phaethornis longuemareus*, perching at a height of nearly a foot above the ground in the dense undergrowth of the rain-forest in Trinidad. The song consisted of a series of rather thin chirping notes.

The singing capabilities of hummingbirds are limited by purely anatomical factors. They have only two muscles controlling the syrinx, the sound-producing organ in birds which is situated right down in the chest where the bronchi branch off from the windpipe. Other species of bird have nine or more muscles, which of course means that with their instrument they can play more developed and complicated tunes.

In Trinidad I met Mrs Margaret Greenewalt who was living in the rain-forest paradise at Spring Hill. She and her husband are close friends of Dr Ruschi, the Brazilian scientist, and with his co-operation Mr Greenewalt wrote his work on hummingbirds, which includes some superb photography. On Mrs Greenewalt's advice I wrote to Dr Ruschi and received in reply an invitation to visit him when I was in Brazil. My visit was an unforgettable experience—a never-ending stream of fairy-tale colour impressions from morning to evening. Dr Ruschi and his family live in a museum, the Museo de Biologia 'Prof. Mello-Leitao' named after his beloved teacher. It is full of live exhibits and is situated in Santa Teresa some miles from the town of Vitoria, an hour's flight from Rio de Janeiro.

On the date arranged we found ourselves at Rio Airport prior to the hop up to Vitoria. While we registered our bulky packages of equipment, I caught sight of a small box which I seemed to recognise. I had seen it and its contents illustrated in the *National Geographic Magazine*. No treasure chest has ever contained finer jewels —this one was full of hummingbirds, packed in rows and wrapped in small pieces of white cloth. A forest of fine bills pointed up at me and small, bright, squirrel-like eyes peered at everything that moved in the vicinity.

Dr Ruschi had just come back from an extensive trip in the Amazon region, and the box contained birds which would be available for physiological and ethnological study. While we talked together in a remarkable blend of languages, in which Portuguese, French, English, German and Latin were represented, Ruschi's hands flew over his delicate treasures, like the wings of a lark, picking each one up in turn and refuelling it from a small bottle containing sugar solution. The varied company stuck their beaks greedily into the bottle. The birds appeared to be completely tame. Shortly, however, I was to see Dr Ruschi feeding hummingbirds in the same matter-of-fact way only a minute after they had been captured. Food is such a vital element in a hummingbird's life that it comes before everything else.

The museum is no fusty, dust-collecting building but rather an airy residence for the masses of birds which are accommodated in a row of cages, one of which is large enough to contain several houses. Hummingbirds from all over Brazil, Venezuela, Ecuador, Peru and many other places live here under natural conditions. Dr Ruschi studies and records them with a devotion which is reflected in the innumerable bulletins which go out to all parts of the world. These publications contain not only descriptions of species and distribution ranges, but also the results of work which must require the precision of a watch-maker. Data may include the body temperatures of the adults and young by night and day, during torpidity and normal sleep; requirements of carbohydrate and protein; incubation periods and the development of the young until fledging; the flight speed and wing-beat frequency of the adults; and, not least, the behaviour during courtship, song, display, mating, nest-building, with some longevity records: indeed everything that it is possible to investigate.

The species which he had caught on the journey included, amongst others, the world's most beautiful hummingbird, *Topaza pella*, in which the male is endowed with a golden patch under the chin and under the rump. The tail and wings are yellow-brown, the breast is reddish-violet, and it has a pair of long dark tail feathers that are crossed. The female lacks these long adornments but parades in green, pink, blue and orange. Together they make a handsome pair.

The cages contain certain rarities but almost more enchanting is the free-living population in the park. At least thirty species of hummingbird are represented. It would be impossible to count all the individuals but some twenty pounds of sugar are used every day in the feeding-bottles which hang everywhere in the trees. The bottles contain a 15% solution, which gives around 14 gallons, sufficient to cover the daily requirements of 3,800 hummingbirds of the size of *Lophornis*. This means that perhaps 2,000 birds are fed daily within the area of the park. The sound of humming on Ruschi's veranda during the afternoon, where a dozen bottles hang, is so loud that one has to raise one's voice to be heard above the whirring of perhaps a score of pairs of wings.

I filmed a large number of species at the food containers and at the numerous specially selected flowers in the park. The most entertaining little bird was *Lophornis*, which is not only the size of a bumble-bee but also buzzes like one. In addition it has a pale band immediately above the brownish tail, which gives it the appearance of a bumble-bee and makes it possible to mistake it for one. Whether it is the sound, the appearance, or some other factor, I do not know, but when this little brown bird with its red cap turns up at a feeding-bottle the large species generally move away.

One day I was lucky enough to witness the courtship display of a male *Lophornis* through the viewfinder of my camera. A small male hovered in a rocking motion, dancing in front of a female in ever tighter semi-circles. The female was so bewitched that she just sat there and almost let him achieve the final stage of courtship. When he dropped down on to the female's back, however, she hummed away, closely pursued by the male. They flew rapidly into the air, perhaps sixty feet high, before dropping down as fast again into the vegetation.

Some days later on a small path I saw the fast-winged *Calliphlox*, the species which has 80 wing-beats per second. It was moving at full speed straight at me; it then braked abruptly, went into reverse for about thirty feet, braked again, and so on time after time. In the middle of this long series of manœuvres the bird drew attention to itself by a rattling probably produced with the help of the tail-feathers. The object of his passion, therefore, must have been somewhere in the vicinity.

The full firework display of the gaudy species is at its best during the courtship of a female. Unfortunately this can only be enjoyed to the full from the angle at which the female sees it. This is because the male positions himself so that the female and the sun are in front of him, within quite a narrow angle. A hummingbird only really sparkles with colour when seen from certain angles and at any other it may appear quite black. The iridescence arises in much the same way as that of a drop of oil on a water surface, where the colours also change with the angle of vision. When I was filming hummingbirds I used one or two lamps and in this way managed to get a 'black' bird to sparkle in lilac, blue and green, a sight that one has few opportunities to see in normal lighting.

Santa Teresa is an agricultural area, but not far away there is an area where the rain-forest grows undisturbed alongside a fairly broad river. The area is protected and two thousand orchids grow there. Unfortunately they were not in flower at the time of my visit. There were also bromelias everywhere covering the trunks of the trees without actually being parasites. They live largely on energy from the sunshine and water from the humid atmosphere, and their flowers are favourites with hummingbirds.

Augusto Ruschi, or Gutchi as everyone in Santa Teresa seemed to call him, carries a little box and a bamboo rod with him on his field expeditions. The latter is a clumsy-looking catching device. Many thousands of the birds are ringed and when Gutchi sees a bird he wants to check on he goes to work with the rod. Made up of numerous sections, it is capable of being extended sufficiently high to reach the tree-tops. He lowers it carefully towards the flowers where he expects the bird to come. When the thirsty hummingbird arrives, Gutchi catches yet another flying jewel with a finely aimed twitch. The tip of the rod has previously been dipped in an extremely sticky substance which holds the bird fast. The rod is quickly dismantled and the bird carefully released. After this the feathers are cleaned with petrol, the bird is held by the bill for a short time while it flutters its wings, effectively fanning away the cleaning liquid. Then it is given a sip out of a small bottle with a seductive red opening. It takes the liquid greedily, showing no sign of alarm. This lack of fear continued to surprise me each time another hummingbird was captured. One can only assume that the birds were slaves to drink.

On one of the occasions when I was filming the catching technique, something took place which I had always hoped to see. Gutchi had already got the rod in its extended position. Looking down for a moment I saw a wasp, a shining bluish insect the size of one's little finger; it was wandering about on the ground evidently on the track of some insect. After touching the ground with its antennae it moved rapidly forwards on a zigzag course. I drew the attention of Gutchi to the wasp and then concentrated again on the tip of the rod and the filming. Suddenly I heard Gutchi shout:

'She's got a spider!'

Sure enough, only twelve to fifteen feet away from us, one of the most exciting natural dramas was being enacted, a struggle between a wasp and a spider. I directed the camera towards the scene of action and got the protagonists in my viewfinder. The whole of the dramatic conflict was played out accompanied by the camera's whirring.

A bird-eating spider stood with its legs raised in front of the blue insect, which faced it with waving antennae and a nervously twitching abdomen. This spider has enough venom to kill a small child and eight powerful legs with which to hold its prey. Its movements are as quick as lightning as I knew from having watched a related species catching large moths. The moths were caught as they fluttered with a leap that was as swift as though the spider had been shot from a catapult. The action was far too quick for the eye to discern details.

Now the wasp suddenly rushed under the giant spider and turned on its back; there was an extremely brief twitching struggle and then the fight was over. The wasp had deposited its sting in the centre of the spider, between its eight legs. The wasp then withdrew its weapon and stepped back a few paces. The spider staggered and fell on its side. The wasp was uninjured and after cleaning itself for a moment it returned to the attack, delivering another sting; there was a further pause and then it gave the spider the *coup de grâce*.

The wasp proceeded to drag the body of the large spider a distance of more than thirty feet over stones and twigs. The spider was only paralysed and its last pair of legs was still capable of functioning, but it was unable to put up any struggle as it had lost control of its body, and its legs, when they moved, only jerked its body farther in the direction of the hole. There it was to be left and slowly eaten, while still alive but paralysed, by the wasp larva which would shortly hatch out. After the wasp had succeeded in getting the spider to the right place, it would deposit an egg on the spider's hairy body. Underlying this vicious struggle is a strong maternal instinct.

This was only one of the many exciting moments of concentrated drama which Ruschi sees repeatedly in his work as a zoologist. But whatever dramas take place in nature I believe that for Ruschi nothing can match the excitement of his daily work, his search for cause and effect, and his passionate interest in the fascinating lilliputian world of the flying jewels.

# 11 *The world's largest turtle*

Sometimes manna falls unexpectedly from heaven and the film-maker is presented with an entire episode in an animal's life, such as the fight between the wasp and the spider which took place when I was staying with Ruschi. These incidents are usually unpredictable and if the camera happens to be already loaded and in position one is lucky. More often than not the story has to be told on film by fitting sequences together to give an impression of continuity in the animal world. The sequences may be the result of filming on various occasions, and scenes may even be taken at yearly intervals, but always with the same background.

After my visit to Brazil and to various other islands I always went back to Trinidad. I was thus able to follow up various changes in different natural processes and by making it my base I felt at home there, something which I find necessary to get everything into perspective. Sometimes one can film to a carefully planned schedule or

*On Curaçao a colony of Cayenne terns nest so close together on a small island in a salt lagoon that the birds—about 4,000 of them—cover almost the whole surface.*
OVERLEAF LEFT *The leatherback turtle has been heaved over the right way up but even in this position it is still in a weak state. The leatherback turtle's eggs are soft and the size of a billiard ball. The three-foot deep pit is dug with stereotyped movements by the long, flexible hind limbs.*
RIGHT *At night-time on Matura Beach the atmosphere is eerie—a scene of habitual crime where many leatherback turtles are killed every year.*

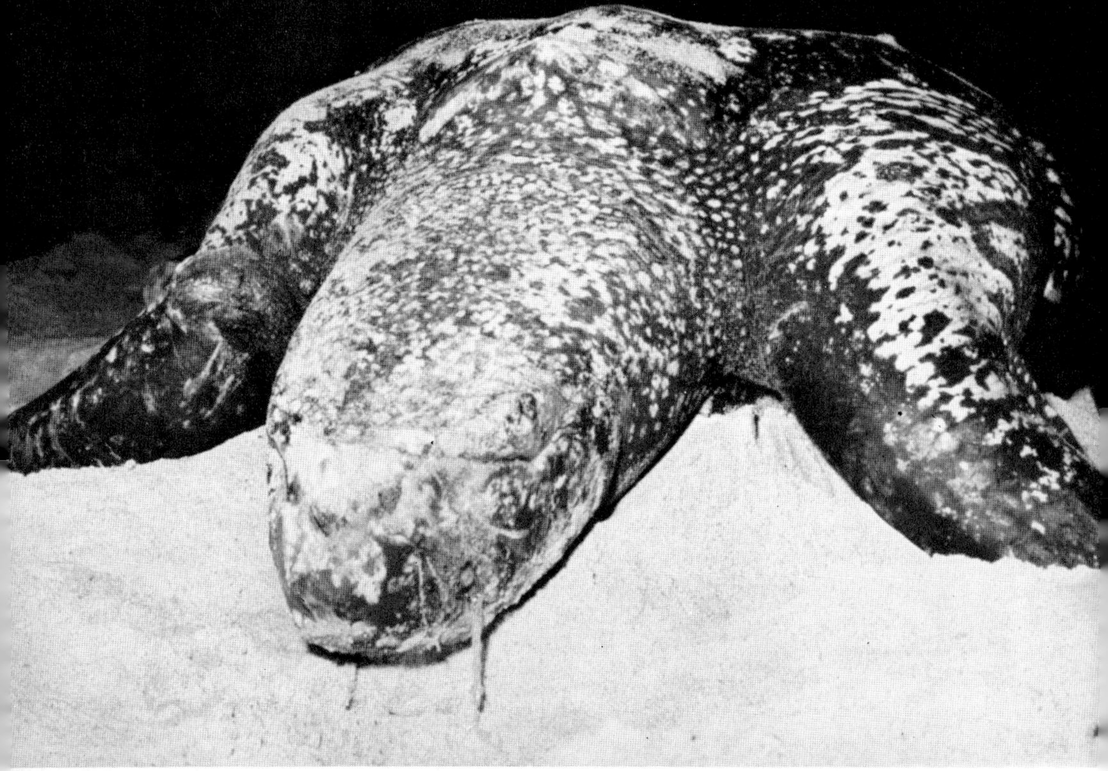

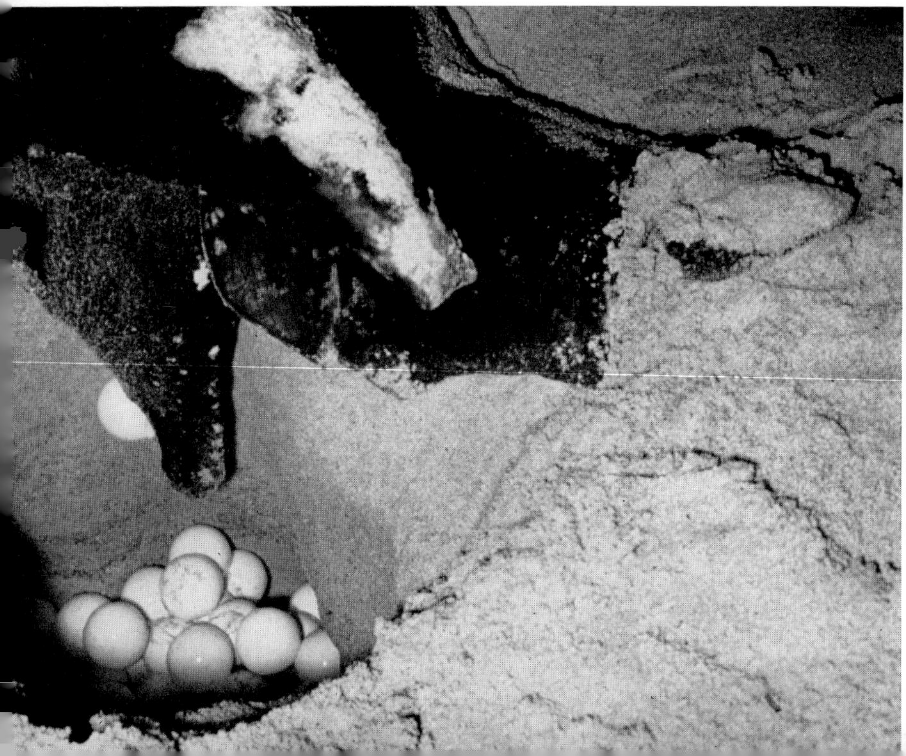

even to a prepared script; at other times, however, things turn out very differently from one's original ideas. This is what happened, for instance, when I tried to get the world's largest turtle on to film.

The leatherback turtle, *Dermochelys coriacea*, is a truly substantial hunk: from nose to tail it may measure 100 inches and its weight reaches a good 1,450 pounds, which is the maximum confirmed weight, although figures of a ton or more have been recorded. It would have been a mistake for nature to try to pack this giant body into the ordinary hard shell of the type found in the other turtles. If a wave carried such a heavy burden on to rocks like those at the approach to St Giles, the turtle would be hurled backwards and forwards and the hard shell would undoubtedly break.

We think of Mother Nature as shrewd and able to cope with widely varying situations. Early on, perhaps as long ago as the early Cretaceous period or perhaps even the Triassic, this turtle developed in a form which remains almost unchanged to this day. The gigantic dorsal shield consists of a thick, tough skin stretched over bone. Seven longitudinal ridges act like the ribs in a boat. The underside is also covered by the same material, stretched over only five bony ridges. The shield or carapace is saturated with an oil which was formerly used as a type of varnish for boats.

Among systematists discussion is still going on as to whether there is a single species of leatherback turtle or whether there are two subspecies, one in the Atlantic and the other in the Pacific. Since these reptiles are extremely rare it has probably not been possible to collect sufficient data on which to base a reliable conclusion.

Leatherback turtles wander widely throughout the tropical seas but the places where the females come ashore to lay are few. The western

*The marine toad,* Bufo marinus, *can reach a length of 5½ inches. The male's territorial song is a long, melodic series of notes which attracts the even larger female (above). The longish glands along the back of the head contain an extremely powerful poison, which can kill a dog if it bites the toad.*

population has been reported from Costa Rica, rarely from Florida and Jamaica, and occasionally also from different islands in the Caribbean Sea. Perhaps the majority of the females go ashore during the egg-laying season to a short strip of beach on the east coast of Trinidad. Matura Beach, where the leatherback turtles deposit their eggs in the sand during May and June, is approximately two miles long. The coast, particularly by moonlight, has an uncanny, ghostly feeling. The dead trees form themselves into tormented shapes, twisted beings with limbs so like human remains that one imagines them to be malefactors who have been condemned and changed into petrified trees—rightly condemned because surely nothing can be more detestable than the murder of a mother giving birth. Since long ago the wretched turtles have been hacked to pieces on the beach by gangs of men, armed with sharp knives, who overpower the animals and turn them on to their backs.

In early May I had the good fortune to see three leatherback turtles in all, making their trip ashore to perpetuate the species. Unfortunately the battery-driven searchlights were troublesome and one night, when everything was set up to film this egg-laying colossus, the battery gave up and the light died away. This was just before I went to Bonaire.

On my return to Trinidad I resumed the attempt to film the egg-laying at night. The season was really over for the turtles but I had heard that individual females were sometimes late breeders and so I persisted doggedly. Elliot Olton, one of the boys who worked in the textile factory at Arima and who had accompanied me on my trips in the rain-forest, was always keen to go with me on these nocturnal expeditions, in spite of the fact that they sometimes took the whole night. We toiled back and forth along the spooky coast, which, in addition to the black tree skeletons, was now garnished by a great many corpses: the remains of turtles slaughtered while laying their eggs. The only form of life to be seen on this dead coast was a white crab. As we approached, the crabs scuttled away from the last remains of the turtles, tripping along on a zigzag course.

At last one night the event which I almost ceased to hope for took place. It was moonlight as Elliot and I walked along the coast. We passed through the barrier of swampy grass which was full of the clanging, whistling, squeaking and croaking voices of frogs and toads. We were accompanied by hordes of the most blood-thirsty and irritating mosquitoes I had ever experienced, worse even than the races in Lapland. The insect repellant we had rubbed on our bodies had probably never been tested out on these examples of Trinidad's horrors, and I believe the brutes regarded the contents of the bottle as an apéritif before dinner. Every time I brushed the clinging mass of insects from my arms and took out the mosquito oil, the devils collected around, happy and high-spirited, hiccuping and yodelling.

At last we were out on the beach and in spite of the scene of carnage found it quite pleasant. The breeze on the shore was warm and strong, and the last mosquito was blown away. We began our usual patrolling along the edge of the tide, hardly exchanging a word. Every now and again the cloud cover parted to reveal the moon; the light varied from a bluish-white half-light to dismal darkness. Sudden rain showers came down like bursts of machine-gun fire, making our route march with the equipment seem ever more senseless. In addition to film cameras, still cameras, flash equipment, two battery-driven searchlights, tripod and film, our packages also contained umbrellas: an incongruous touch to an already remarkable sight.

We wandered backwards and forwards along the shore for seven hours, the slippery sand making the sound of the surf that much more conducive to sleep at one o'clock in the morning. Then we stopped and listened. Something was coming ashore. At last we were to be rewarded. We forgot all about our discomfort and the strain on our backs of the heavy packs.

There have been occasions in my life when I have suddenly had the feeling of being able to look back over long periods of time and to see thousands and thousands of years all linked together: as in the hide at a crane's nest on the moors with the bird's bronze Viking horns sounding in the first light of dawn, or when the female eagle owl came gliding in silently over the cliff towards her snapping young. But the feeling had never been as strong as that night on the beach, watching the turtle heading for land. In the pale blue moonlight at the edge of the water, where the sea foam sensuously licks the smooth sand, a colossus comes ashore. A few laboured strokes of the giant flippers and a snorting groan can be heard clearly above the continuous sound of the wind in the mangroves behind us and the booming of the waves out in the silvery sea. She is carried slowly in, no graceful Aphrodite but a big shining box-like creature, going up and down with the water which pours off the rough texture of her body at the sides. The surging water lets go of her and as she moves up the beach she follows a course which will lead her past us. We stand stock still like living replicas of the black tree skeletons.

Her characteristic trail lies printed in the sand—a broad tractor track made by the heavy body and the big paddles. Her head is raised, the bulging pocket of skin beneath her chin is emptied and her huge lungs take in another breath; with a groan she sinks down, her head resting on the sand; she lies there completely still for a long time. In the water she is a skilful swimmer, on land she becomes like a gigantic rock, like an astronaut on Jupiter weighed down by the force of gravity. She makes another effort, plodding slowly on until she reaches that part of the shore suitable for laying her eggs. My tired body now glows with a sense of triumph. At last the turtle can be filmed.

Then something happens: the giant turtle gets stuck under one of the distorted trees. She lies there, a recumbent idol with sinewy arms, held by the petrified shape of the skeleton tree. The whole tree quivers as the malicious spirit appears to hold her in an iron grip. But the turtle is strong and she thrusts her body forwards, using her yard-long paddles. The tree gives way and with a falsetto squeal loses a long branch, which falls down on to the turtle's back with a rattle of dry wood.

The turtle lies quite still, not injured but frightened. Five, perhaps ten, long minutes go by. The waves are washing over our feet, the sand gives way under them, and once again we are aware of the straps cutting into our bodies from the weight of our packs. The mood of triumph gives way to one of hopeless resignation as the turtle turns round and heads for the sea, making as much speed as when she came ashore. When she reaches the sparkling sea she turns southwards and we walk along towards the part of the beach where there is just a faint chance that she might come ashore again. It is not easy to spot her among the lines of surf, only her head appearing as a flashing black disc.

It is now high tide and the moon, which is not yet full, has passed its highest point. Sun and moon, each in its own position, exert a pull on the earth's water masses, trying in vain to cover up the nakedness of the shore. We wander on while keeping a permanent watch along the seaboard, dodging the worst of the waves. Out on a projecting sand-bank we see the dark box again, raising itself up out of the surf as the foam slides away. And so after only half an hour, the turtle is ready to come ashore again.

All is well and we hang up our rucksacks on the branches of a dead mangrove bush and wait patiently for the landing: our last hope. But our troubles are not over. Something incredible happened next and at first I did not understand what was going on. It started with an uncomfortable rocking sensation, like the beginning of car-sickness. Then a couple of powerful, soft thrusts came up under our feet, followed by another couple. The rocking movement lasted perhaps fifteen, twenty seconds. The water gushed up in a huge swell, nearly making us lose our balance; swirling on, it moved towards our rucksacks in the tree. It was an earthquake, the first I had ever experienced. The turtle was swept away. At five o'clock we abandoned our watch, dead tired.

The next day, however, my hopes began to rise again. The weather was exceptionally bad and there was no doubt that this was the rainy season. For the first part of our expedition to the beach we had to use a car and found the starter would not work. Elliot's brother, who had heard about the previous day's turtle and wanted to come with us, helped to start up the car by hand and we drove off in lashing rain. I was half-resigned to another failure but deep down I had a glowing conviction that the turtle would turn up somewhere, however unsuitable the weather. There were perhaps 150 eggs confined in her oviduct and she would be forced to come ashore.

We arrived having passed through the barrage of mosquitoes and quickly arranged ourselves into three patrols. I hurried off between the trees, this time with no pack on my back. Then I saw a lamp shining ahead and this made me worried.

Had we arrived three minutes later we would not only have been too late to film but too late to save the life of the turtle. A gang of seven men were in the very act of turning the turtle on to her back. Once she was on her back they would merely cut off her head and limbs and thrust their long bush-knives into the groaning body.

She fell over on her back, and her big, sweeping fin-like paddles forced the men to retire rapidly. They were dancing backwards and forwards, the moonlight glinting on their knife blades, ready to aim the first blow. I let out a yell and rushed forwards. I tried to convince them that this particular animal had long since been reserved for filming purposes and that I had been sent there by the government. The government was always a good wicket in a number of different situations. I spoke of how strictly the authorities were now punishing offences against the protection laws, and laid a trail of other white lies. In fact the leatherback turtle is not protected at all.

It was naturally not possible to make the gang accept my arguments but after a certain amount of bargaining I managed to buy the turtle for filming for twenty dollars. This was all the money that I had on me. After receiving the agreed light signal my three companions came up quickly with all the equipment. Lying on the ground, looking like a tall sea-chest from the turn of the century, the turtle was waving her paddles impotently, wasting energy in trying to right herself. The sand shot up into the air like fireworks. She looked almost more impressive in this position.

We got ready for filming on the assumption that all we could now expect to film was her clumsy walk down to her true element. A terror-stricken colossus in retreat, not a remarkable subject for film but something by way of consolation for the ruin of our plans by an irresponsible gang of men. The prospect of waiting for yet another week on the ever-decreasing chance of getting a further opportunity to film was not a very attractive one.

I filmed the men turning the giant female over, right side up, with the aid of long bamboo poles. It required all their strength. I then ran eagerly down to the water's edge, accompanied by Elliot's brother, who was carrying the searchlights. We waited and waited. I was seized by misgivings. By then the turtle should have been half-way down the beach. The noise of the wind and the sea was so loud that any shouts from the men would have been drowned. Had one of them been unable to resist chopping her head off even now?

I had almost decided to run back again when Elliot came rushing up. 'She's digging!' he said breathlessly. The turtle had been prevented from laying her eggs for a whole twenty-four hours and was now forced to get rid of them. Like a gigantic computerised machine she went through the whole of her programme. The flexible tip of one hind-paddle sank down into the sand behind the tail and started to dig. After about six digging movements a small portion of sand held in the paddle scoop was lifted up and at the same time the other paddle was lowered. When this one was fully loaded the upper scoop threw its load of sand backwards with a jerk. Everything was perfectly co-ordinated for producing a pit three feet deep in the tidiest possible way. She was making a hole in the sand destined to be a strong-room for keeping the precious eggs safe. The job is done with remarkable precision, perfected after millions of years of trial and error, according to a plan of action built into certain combinations of genes which now function automatically and instinctively.

The way in which an animal with no intelligence will follow an instinctive pattern is both fascinating and impressive. I could not help being moved by the sight of this ugly, awkward reptile, so helpless in its strength, so fixed in its purpose. She went on scooping out the sand until the paddles could no longer reach the bottom of the pit. She then had a rest, taking long, deep breaths. It was as though the computer were turning out the instructions for the next stage in the programme, the laying of the eggs.

In the meantime the men in the hunting gang had changed their attitude to one of helpfulness. Searchlights, tripod, camera, and shovel were handled with almost military precision. They seemed to find some merit in working for a TV film; perhaps they hoped to see the film later on TTT (Trinidad and Tobago Television). I started to dig a hole behind the turtle's egg pit but the gang took my shovel off me and finished the job in record time. On the other hand they did not seem to be keen on appearing in the film. The one who appeared to be the leader shouted to the others: 'Don't show your faces.' I did not understand then why they should object to having their pictures taken. I went down into my pit and was able to film the egg-laying from a promising angle. 'Labour' started and an egg appeared, pressed slowly out of the cloaca, then another and yet another, until they were produced at a rate which left a pile of shining white eggs the size of billiard balls, lying at the bottom of the pit. Gradually the lower and somewhat narrower part of the pit was filled in with about a hundred and thirty eggs.

Then the turtle took a rest. She lay motionless; now and then the sac under her chin was filled with air which she expelled with a groan.

*We pushed the boat right into the mangroves, which provided an effective camouflage for trying to take pictures of the scarlet ibis—and the poachers in Caroni.*

OVERLEAF LEFT *Nobody goes out into the rain-forest without a cutlass or bush-knife. The people in the mountain districts kill all snakes on sight—understandably because it is difficult to survive the bite from a large fer-de-lance like this one.*

RIGHT *The cattle egret was first seen in Trinidad in 1952. The numbers have now reached several thousands—a real population explosion.*

CENTRE SPREAD *This flock contains about five hundred cattle egrets flying in to their roosting tree at Caroni.*

29

It was as if she were trying to get away from all she was forced to do by instinct. Long, viscous tear-drops hung from her eyes, which blinked regularly, squeezing the tears out. Many people who have described the shedding of tears in marine turtles have been tempted to assume that the process of egg-laying is extremely painful. This is a sentimental interpretation, however, and has no scientific basis of any kind. The true explanation is quite different, less emotional but no less interesting.

The ancestors of the turtles, like our own, left the sea many millions of years ago. Their blood contained a certain amount of salt, and in fact its content was about the same as that of the sea at that time. Like us the turtle has retained this basic information in the gene structure of its reproductive cells, completely unchanged after all those millions of years. During the time that went by before these terrestrial reptiles again returned to the sea, the salt content of the sea had increased considerably, due to the weathering action of precipitation and the washing out of substances from the surfaces of the land. The salt had to be removed from the cells of those animals which returned to their original habitat. This was achieved by excretion from the blood with the help of salt glands. Marine birds with dripping beaks and tear-eyed leatherback turtles show evidence of the same solution of the problem. On land the turtle's 'tears' hang

ABOVE *Winston and I were accompanied by a game ranger. We were out in good time. The poachers generally showed up after nightfall.* BELOW *While waiting we were able to study a multitude of crabs on the mud-banks. There are eight species of fiddler-crab in Trinidad. In all of these the male has a much-enlarged claw, with which it makes sweeping, 'fiddling' movements.*

PREVIOUS TWO PAGES, LEFT *Cattle egrets have for long lived on the numerous insects which thrive around cattle and other large animals. As cattle become scarcer we may have to give this species a new name: tractor egrets might be more appropriate.*

RIGHT *The snowy egrets nest close together among the cattle egrets in the large colonies in Caroni Swamp. During the hottest part of the day the birds often stand panting on the nests, shading their young with half extended wings.*

like globules mixed with sand, while in the sea they are washed away.

The turtle had rested for a long time and meanwhile we had filled in the photographic pit. I filmed this being done and once again the gang's leader warned the men not to show their faces to the camera. When I tried to film the one whom I had already filmed earlier with a bush-knife in his hand, he turned away. The gang spoke a very peculiar version of English. Trinidad has a wide variety of tongues with ingredients from most parts of the world. In effect they argued that I had bought the turtle for filming and the conditions of the contract had now been fulfilled. The purchase price had included the right to film the turtle but not the right to save her life. 'Let the man flim, he didn't asks nothing more.'

While the conversation switched to the epicurean delights of the turtle's liver, the turtle concentrated on hiding her eggs, working away assiduously. Sand was thrown backwards with her three-foot-long front limbs and was trampled down into the hole. Somebody put a stick near one of the poles which had been used to turn her over. The eggs would of course be dug up later. Elliot, who was holding one of the film lamps, managed to remove this marker under cover of the blinding light. The turtle moved around, covering a large area, digging and throwing sand. The eggs were soon out of reach in spite of everything that had happened.

While part of my brain concentrated on the filming, I was also turning over another idea in my mind. The turtle had finished her task and would soon start walking towards the sea, and as the filming was completed the gang would doubtless want to slaughter her.

'You over there,' I said to one of the men, whose hair-style was obviously designed with women in mind. 'You look very like Errol Flynn. It's a pity that you can't star in this film.'

I explained that I would be showing the film in various parts of the world, if not actually in Hollywood, and it seemed a great pity that he should not take part in it. I really needed to film somebody on the turtle's back, someone with good looks and a bold character. After some more flattery the potential film star climbed on to the back of our Aphrodite, who scarcely seemed to notice her burden. I filmed the proud jockey doing his act and suddenly the others decided not to be left out. The thought that they might be engaged in a role opposite some glamorous film star made them forget their leader's warning. Stylish rows of teeth in Indian faces vied with the bright moonlight in brilliance: 'Smile, man, smile!'

After a while they realised I had tricked them. It was true that they would soon be on TV but they would also be identifiable, and if they were to slaughter the turtle now they would later be branded as law-breakers, supported by pictorial evidence. As I backed out into the waves, filming the man as he rode the turtle towards the sea. one searchlight went out and the other only just lasted until the turtle finally returned to the freedom of the seas. After all the excitement we were aching with fatigue. But our luck held and we felt happy and triumphant, for the turtle was safe.

# 12 *The home of the birds of fire*

The protection of nature is something which ought to concern us all because whatever the kind of life we lead or wherever we live we are dependent upon the natural environment. People who understand and appreciate nature to the full are perhaps in the minority today. By the time the natural scene is better appreciated, it may no longer exist. The selfish economic interests of the few dictate a policy that is short-sighted in the long run, and the indifference of the majority is expressed in an attitude of mind which says 'it will all work out in the end.' These arguments provide a shield against which the weapons of nature conservation are either parried or shattered.

Where animals are concerned, the warnings of conservationists usually begin to have an effect on public opinion only when it has become a matter of saving the last few individuals of a remnant population and the survival of the species is already seriously in doubt. All too often it is already too late to save the species, as for instance seems to be the case with eagle owls and peregrine falcons in Sweden, which are suffering from the effects of toxic chemicals. The warning cry of the conservationist takes on the character of a death scream which is invariably drowned by the clatter of machinery and the call for higher standards of living. Everywhere I went on my filming expeditions I was aware of the effects of man's exploitation of nature. His mere presence in the vicinity is often sufficiently destructive to make the end inevitable.

The future survival of the scarlet ibis is seriously in doubt. In Trinidad these birds occur in their thousands and it may well seem too far-fetched to suggest that extermination of the population is imminent. Unfortunately man has shown himself capable of completely destroying the habitat of other animals in a very short space of time, even when a species has been present in large numbers. This has happened many times.

The story of the destruction of the North American passenger pigeon is one of the bloodiest in the history of man's extermination of species and it provides a striking comparison with the present decrease in the scarlet ibis. Around 1800 the passenger pigeon occurred in incredibly large numbers. In 1810 an ornithologist estimated a flock of over two milliards of birds. The species was subject to continual disturbance, and there was no control of any kind on shooting. Nevertheless in 1871 some 136 million of them bred in one single locality. Yet the last wild passenger pigeon was seen in 1899. In less than thirty years therefore man had successfully accomplished a gigantic programme of extermination. The birds were never left in peace and never got the necessary privacy during the nesting season.

The passenger pigeon was a gregarious species unable to breed successfully unless large numbers were present in an undisturbed breeding area. The presence of large numbers was necessary as a form of social stimulus so that each individual could be brought quietly to the stage where it was ready to mate. The scarlet ibis requires similar conditions. When large numbers are left undisturbed they nearly all breed; when disturbed not a single pair will do so. This is surely the secret behind the catastrophic decrease in their numbers during the last fifty years.

How can this species be saved? There is a hydra—the tourist industry—which could be enticed to lay its coils around the bird's future and protect it. With the help of the tourist industry Caroni could be made into the equivalent of an Everglades of the West Indies, as the home of the world's most beautiful bird. It is true that such a development is a depressing thought, with chugging motorboats and loud-voiced guides, noisy coaches, restaurants, long wooden gangways as trails to points of interest, and high look-out towers.

Perhaps, as in the real Everglades, tame alligators could be provided which only expect a slice of bread in exchange for providing people with snapshots. But every possible method should be considered as a means of saving the species for posterity. The most important safeguard of all, however, is that protection should be strictly enforced.

Nocturnal poachers had already been caught during March by the patrols sent out by Mr Murray, the Chief Game Warden. But instead of having their boats and weapons confiscated and their firearm licences withdrawn, they were penalised by ridiculously low fines. Game rangers now patrol the area and carry out inspections at irregular intervals by day and night. This has acted as a moderating influence but not as a complete deterrent. The shooting goes on but never within the Sanctuary. Winston Nanan and I frequently saw hunters but managed to frighten them off by an effective method of our own. We sailed up on them silhouetted against the evening sun and looked at them through field-glasses. I then handled a stick of mangrove as though re-loading a rifle and pointed out a course as though intending to intercept the poachers. The motor went into action with a roar and stopped with a cough. The echo was heard in the mangrove jungle, and the poachers received the start we intended them to have.

When Trinidad and Tobago Television invited me for an interview on their current affairs programme, I showed some film and seized the opportunity to talk about the ibis and its protection. As in Europe, TV in Trinidad is the best means of disseminating news, and I became expansive about the possibilities of infra-red film: I explained that with the aid of the sniperscope I could now see in pitch-darkness and film without a trace of visible light. Perhaps it was coincidence but after this we did not hear a single shot in Caroni. Whatever the reason, the poachers appeared to have left the area.

Television is not purely and simply a news-distributing medium. It also has a powerful influence on public opinion and on the adoption of new attitudes of mind towards nature. Since we no longer need to hunt for food to the same extent as before, the drive to hunt must—like other drives—be sublimated.

Hunting and killing are traditions which have been passed on from generation to generation. An inherited tradition, however, is not the same thing as an instinctive drive, and a new tradition can be built up since the desire to protect and create is at least as strong as that to kill. Television programmes for children and young people carry an unprecedented and also very rewarding responsibility. The excitement of a hunt, with only a camera and tape-recorder as weapons, can give a new impression of the fascination of animal life when it is seen undisturbed. Wildlife can be pursued and recorded objectively, giving pleasure even to those who want to capture everything they see. To watch or to listen, as a mere observer, gives the greatest satisfaction of all: witness the many sportsmen who have turned from hunting to game preservation or even to disinterested conservation of wildlife.

Progress has certainly been made in Europe and all over the world. The traditional stories of big game hunting are for the most part regarded nowadays as manifestations of a bygone age. There are plenty of stories concerning the hunting and persecution of the scarlet ibis. The following example comes from August Kappler's *Six years in Surinam, 1854* (freely translated):

'Eggs and young are highly valued by the Indians who sometimes undertake expeditions to the nesting sites. One day my neighbours came by in two big canoes on their way to collect eggs. After I had offered them brandy they promised to give me a basketful. Some days later the two canoes returned fully loaded with eggs and young. They gave me about a hundred eggs, which were greenish with black markings and the size of a hen's egg. I started to make an omelette, but to my disappointment found that only one egg out of the whole batch was fresh. All the others were rotten or at an advanced stage of incubation. I suspected that the Indians had been making fun of me. Having abandoned the idea of eating an omelette, I went into the town where I found a woman in the middle of cooking eggs. They were all in the same state as mine. Bird embryos at various stages of development were floating in a soup of egg-yolks and, copiously laced with Spanish pepper, this dish was eaten voraciously.'

The same lover of omelettes boasted that he had shot seventeen scarlet ibises with one shot. The pioneers of our civilisation certainly distinguished themselves. It is almost as horrible as an obituary written by another author:

'As the guns went off the birds in the immediate vicinity were frightened into the air and became a huge flock on the wing; the adult birds circled round and round, as though too bewildered to understand the danger they instinctively feared. In this way they offered magnificent targets for our skill and the beach near the canoe was soon strewn with fine specimens.'

This took place during the breeding season and the birds that were shot had young in the nest. Today most of us feel nauseated by such gruesome accounts, and this at least is a healthy sign. In former times such stories were accepted without any sense of disgust.

I built a number of platforms and hides at various places in Caroni in order to film the egrets at their nests. This kind of work always strikes some instinctive chord in me. Like the gorilla, which undoubtedly finds great satisfaction in making his sleeping nest in a suitable tree, I feel at home when I rig up a green hide, whether in a swaying spruce in Sweden or in the mangroves of Caroni. The happiness I feel when I am resting on a hard platform surrounded by

*As though at a given signal all the ibises in the flock cease to flap their wings and glide with a soft murmur through the air for a few seconds before beating their wings again and disappearing among the mangroves. Like flames of living fire the scarlet ibises dive down into the mangroves beneath the last rays of the setting sun.*
CENTRE SPREAD *Wave after wave of ibises, over three thousand of them in a period of 15 to 20 minutes, come in to settle down in the enormous mangrove tree. An orgy of blood-red which is one of the seven wonders of the bird world.*

worthwhile sights and sounds cannot be compared with anything else—except perhaps when I am swinging gently in a hammock, slung beneath a tarpaulin low down in a tree surrounded by hundreds of birds. The breeze is refreshingly cool, the stars sparkle in the slight ripple on the water and gaze down at me through the holes in the canvas and openings in the foliage, which is full of sleeping birds. One can hear thousands of soft plops, like a tap dripping at intervals, as the droppings of birds fall into the water. Everything is quiet and peaceful.

The sounds which accompany my vigil are characteristic and tell the time like a clock. The ibis flocks move in during the last half-hour before sunset and drop chattering and fluttering into the foliage above. Snowy egrets and cattle egrets come diving into the trees, keeping up a noisy running commentary. Now and then the voices of the tricoloured heron cut through the other sounds and finally the little blue herons begin their scarcely melodious trumpet concert.

This moderately tuneful chorus of song dies down as the sky becomes bluer and the hoarse calls of night-herons can be heard echoing through the trees. As the sounds gradually die away leaving an empty silence one can hear in the distance the long-drawn-out call of the potoo: 'Oh-poor-me-one.' It is a final exhortation to slumber, accompanied by the high-pitched sounds of insects. Here the insects do nothing worse than make music and there is not one mosquito out on a nocturnal hunt. The conditions are unsuitable for those stinging insects as the water is too salt, and I have never needed a mosquito net in the trees at Caroni.

Dawn comes stealthily, with the first precursor around half past four, when the birds start their morning toilet in the dark. The wing-feathers are drawn through the bill, the whole body surface is gone

*After an interval of three years, during which nesting colonies were disturbed by the activities of nocturnal poachers, the scarlet ibis has been able to nest once again in Caroni Swamp in Trinidad.*

over, and now and again there is a loud rustle as their feathers are shaken. It is too dark to see anything of this, but the long microphone cables carry the information to my earphones through the tape-recorder. The potoo begins to wake up, the woodrails start their strident strumming, egrets and ibises make sharp little contributions. The big flocks of rice-grackles, black passerines the size of a blackbird which occupy small mangrove bushes throughout the swamp, begin a monosyllabic song which gradually becomes polyphonic and finally sounds like a busy river. The sky changes quickly from indigo to paler blue, then to the colour of ox blood, and to ibis scarlet, and the morning flight of red, white and blue birds starts from the mangrove trees. The sun soon rises, lighting up the long bands of ibises on the move in an indescribably brilliant colour. Often some hundreds of birds drop into knee-deep water and bathe energetically, creating an effect like the fluttering flames of many fires. Clapper-rails burst into activity with a series of explosive claps, snowy egrets and little blue herons wade slowly in the brownish-black water searching hungrily for food with outstretched necks, and a tricoloured heron quickly catches a fish during its promenade upstream. A new day has begun.

The ibis is without doubt the most beautiful of the species present in Trinidad but it has a close rival in the roseate spoonbill. This bird does not actually breed in Trinidad, in spite of the fact that all its natural requirements are found there. Each year some of them inspect the area. On two occasions while I was there ten birds arrived together and stayed for some weeks but soon moved away on smelling gunpowder from the poachers' guns. If Caroni were to become an undisturbed, protected place, these pink birds with their wine-red wing patches and golden-yellow tails would certainly be one of the first immigrants.

One of the birds which moved off as a result of the outburst of shooting which took place during the spring was the egret *Casmerodius albus egretta,* usually known in Trinidad as 'the big American.' This species nests from time to time amongst the snowy egrets and cattle egrets. Over three hundred hung around for a while at one of the large colonies.

The cattle egrets, unlike other species, do not yield ground in the face of man's progress. When one sees thousands of these birds in Caroni it is difficult to believe that some years ago they caused a big sensation for their rarity. The cattle egret was first seen in Trinidad in 1952 and can rightly be regarded as a population explosion species. The flock was driven across the Atlantic by wind. It came from Africa and turned up in 1930 in British Guiana (now Guyana). Immigration from the Old World probably occurs all the time. One specimen, ringed in Spain, was found the following year in Trinidad.

North America has also been annexed by this successful immigrant, and during my year in Trinidad the species turned up in California, thus reaching the Pacific coast. At the same time it has spread eastwards, and New Guinea and Australia are among the areas it has invaded. New Zealand had a single individual in 1963, another specimen arrived the same year and during the next season there were five in all. It is difficult to say precisely why the cattle egret is so successful but I believe that the most important single factor, strangely enough, is man and his technical developments.

The efficiency of modern agricultural machinery has opened a new ecological niche. The new ploughs, drawn by powerful tractors, now work as efficiently in the sugar plantations of Trinidad as in other agricultural districts of the world. The cattle egrets eat the vast quantities of worms and insects brought to the surface. Egrets feed largely on insects and other small forms of animal life and are very rarely seen fishing for food. The only limiting factor to the spread of the cattle egret may well be the climate. We might eventually see these small white egrets in South Sweden, though the niche there is at present filled by gulls. During the last decades gulls have been changing their habits rapidly, abandoning their fishing and going in for agriculture. Nowadays it is the black-headed gull which is particularly linked with agricultural habitats.

The cattle egrets in Caroni may find their food on the land, but they have chosen the traditional egret haunts as a nesting area. This means that they have quite long journeys to and from their feeding areas, sometimes travelling over twelve miles. In the nesting area they have moved in together with the snowy egrets, a species that feeds primarily by fishing and shows no interest at all in feeding on land. Little blue herons and tricoloured herons are also found nesting in these trees, which often look like giant toadstools dotted with nests, reminiscent of the spots on a fly agaric.

The noise during the extended nesting season is fantastic. Egrets do not belong among the more peaceable birds, and squabbling and scolding seem to be the order of the day. The guttural croaks are mostly associated with squabbles over nesting materials, for the egrets impudently steal twigs from each other. Paradoxically the crime serves a useful purpose, since if nest-building were not kept in check the tree would soon be choked by the masses of nests and would die. As it is each twig is used again and again, the antiques being passed from family to family.

It was a huge task trying to keep track of the nesting progress of all the different species of egret. I hoped of course that the ibises would also start to breed. As I have mentioned there were no signs of the earlier intensive shooting, for the game ranger patrols seemed to have this under control. An incident did occur, however, which reminded us that although the poachers had gone into hiding they were by no means inactive. One evening after Winston had collected me from the hide, I lay stretched out in the boat on one of the seats, watching the parade of stars twinkling down through the tree-tops as we moved along the channels. We were making quite good speed when suddenly the boat heeled over and was thrown to one side by a twisting movement. Camera bags, tape-recorder and other things all shifted violently as the engine of the boat suddenly roared, but remarkably enough nothing fell into the water. A big mangrove pole had been driven down in the centre of the channel which we normally used. The angle at which it sloped was not without a certain finesse in reckoning the result.

At the beginning of August I began to notice certain promising signs among the ibises. Normally these birds fly quite low and fast. Now I occasionally saw them in pairs sailing hundreds of feet up, tumbling around and turning in circles on rigid wings and flying down to the mangrove clumps around the old nesting area. I also saw whole flocks displaying in the same manner.

The giant 'centre' tree, where the poachers had perpetrated their slaughter on the memorable evening in March, now began to attract more and more of these brilliant scarlet birds. At the same time it was clear that many of the egrets had finished rearing their chicks, for many of their nests were empty and undoubtedly served as a big attraction to the ibises. According to several observers in the second half of the nineteenth century, when these birds were extremely common throughout their distribution range, the scarlet ibises took over the nests of certain species of egret. One writer went as far as to say that in general they never built their own nests.

By now the ibises were in gaudy red plumage and as each day went by the evening invasion of the trees became more and more spectacular as the foliage was drowned by a tornado of red wings. The branches of the 'centre' tree, which alone accommodated over three thousand scarlet ibises every night, shone like clusters of rowan berries. The evening flight to the trees, which usually occurred during the last fifteen minutes of sunshine, now started to take place earlier. Large flocks were already arriving around five o'clock, some over an hour earlier. Instead of a short period of nasal conversation just before the light faded there was a continuous series of displays. The birds often stood facing each other, threatening with their bills and beating their wings as they tottered about on the thin branches and ducked in and out of the canopy of leaves. My observation point in a bush about 150 yards from the tree unfortunately did not allow me to see the detail of the pattern of behaviour which probably preceded mating. No mating was actually seen but perhaps this takes place at the nest.

On 25th August, perhaps ten birds in all remained in the tree for the whole day, and after this the number increased. The intensive watch kept by Mr Murray's men was most effective, for the birds, completely free from disturbance, now started to breed. Unfortunately I was not able to follow the build-up of the red legions through the nesting season of the ibises as I was forced to go on another filming trip. I did not return until the beginning of October, after Winston Nanan wrote to say that the nesting would soon be over.

The tree which had supported thousands of ibises now only had hundreds. They shone in the foliage like solitary beacons, and the former carpet of red ibises was no longer to be seen. The nesting of this rare bird had aroused further activity on the human front and these shy animals had once more dispersed. The causes were many. Short-sighted and careless handling of the delicate situation in various ways had broken up the promise of a good breeding season. Seven thousand birds had been present but the young were numbered only in hundreds. The damage had already been done for want of proper protection.

So as to film the birds during the nesting period and to record not only the behaviour of the adults in relation to the young but also the little known earlier stages following pair-formation, I had brought with me a special lens weighing 20 pounds. Compared with the normal lens it gave an enlargement of 24 times. As no new pairs seemed to be arriving at the tree, I decided not to build my hide in the mangroves at a distance of 150 yards but to erect a photographic tower close to the colony.

The tower was put up in short shifts over a period of nine days. I chose the side of the tree where only a few birds had their nests and only two or three of these could be seen from the tower. This was camouflaged by the growth of the green mangrove branches and from the birds' point of view seemed to grow up as part of the tree itself. The birds were not alarmed by any banging; Winston, Elliot and I assembled the whole thing without uttering a single word and immediately after each building shift we left the scene and disappeared completely.

Working from this elevated hide meant that I could get an insight into the family life of the ibises while the birds were totally unaware of my presence. I spent four days on the first story of the tower and three days on the second story. I felt rather like James Bond spying on a colony of Reds and my system of espionage was meticulously planned. The master spy himself would not have had much to add in the way of espionage equipment. A ciné camera and a still camera were placed on each of the two stories. The tape-recorder worked with microphones fastened to mangrove poles, which were directed towards important centres of information. I was also able to pick up special sounds with the parabolic reflector when and where this was necessary. All agents have a contact man at a discreet distance and accordingly I kept in touch with Winston through a walkie-talkie, which was only used when the time came for me to break off my observations after an indeterminate number of days. Silence and care are indeed the alpha and omega both for James Bond and for an agent spying on birds. In both cases failure to observe these golden rules may have fatal results. Lack of care at a nest with young endangers the life of the chicks. Loading of cameras must be done silently, every piece of equipment must be set up in its correct position from the start and all movements between these various work stations must take place with a slowness that would make a snail stamp with impatience. Sandwiches and other food must be packed in material that does not rustle, while people who snore are clearly unsuitable for the role of spy. In my case of course the nights as well as the days were filled with opportunities to observe the behaviour of the birds, for no agent has any definite hours of work.

The name of James Bond is by no means unfamiliar in this part of the world. On the contrary it means something real to travellers to the West Indies who are interested in birds because James Bond is the author of *Birds of the West Indies*. (The new edition has excellent colour pictures by my friend Don Eckelberry.) Ian Fleming thought the name so striking that he annexed it for his hero. James Bond the author is said to be quite happy about lending his name, for he now gets a lot of amusement from the surprised faces of customs officers and porters. He is alleged to be thinking of taking his own form of revenge and it would not be surprising if one day a subspecies of some West Indian bird came to be known under the subspecific name, *flemingi*.

As soon as the hide was ready, with cameras and all the other equipment in place, Winston punted the boat away. The birds now returned to their nests and through my spy-hole the telephoto lens was focused on images of an incredible red. This was the first time I had seen the ibises at such close quarters, at a distance of only seven or eight yards. They did not seem to notice me at all, but stood in a sleeping position with the long bill tucked between the wings. Their plumage shone like silk and gleamed like a purple-red royal mantle. It was a remarkably beautiful sight and the effect of luminosity was increased as the sunlight disappeared and the insect orchestra began to tune up.

No bird can hope to survive in such an ostentatious dress if it remains on its own. Other brilliant colours in bird plumages often seem to serve as camouflage when the bird is in its natural surroundings, for a bright blue or green bird seems to disappear against a certain type of background. But there is every chance that a blood-red bird with a backcloth of green will catch the eye of, for instance, a bird of prey. It is only the gregarious habits of the ibises that can save them. For some reason a bird of prey never seems able to take a member of a well-knit group of birds. If isolated scarlet ibises tried to nest, predators would soon kill them and destroy their nests. The strength of the ibis as a species lies in numbers, but this is also its weakness from the point of view of human disturbance.

I settled myself for the night on my platform and the special feeling of being at home high up in my own nest came over me. The chirping from grasshoppers was interspersed with the usual night heron calls. Sleepy egret commentaries accompanied the begging calls of the night heron chicks from the interior of the tree. Gradually the feeble reflections of the stars in the water took on a sparkling brilliance; everything seemed much nearer and sounds that came from far away sounded quite close.

Suddenly I heard an extremely feeble sound which did not belong to the ordinary repertoire of sounds—then again—and yet again, distinctly closer. I turned slowly round on my floor of planks and lifted up one of the tent flaps. The sound was there again—a pole against the side of a boat—and slowly a silhouette disengaged itself from the dark background of the mangroves about a hundred yards away. The shadow came closer, and I was able to make out two figures in the boat. They moved incredibly quietly as though taking care not to wake someone sleeping. I thought of Winston's report of how one night his family's boats were smashed to bits by poachers, in revenge for Winston's father having reported them.

I already had proof that my involvement in the affairs of the nocturnal hunters was not completely to their liking, and I now found myself trapped in a tree like an animal. Here they would have every opportunity of paying off old scores. All my equipment was on the platform. Apart from being expensive and in many cases irreplaceable, it provided my sole means of carrying on my work.

The boat came straight ahead, creeping towards the tower. I groped my way to the tool box and stealthily drew out a kitchen knife and a penknife which I opened at the largest blade. Without any clear plan of action in my head I knelt down over the entrance hole to the platform. I had no idea what would happen but I was determined not to allow anyone near my valuable possessions.

The boat came straight in under the steel tubing of the tower and one of the men got up slowly and said in a whisper:

'Is everything all right, Mr Lindblad?'

Suddenly the situation became farcical and I was glad that the men could not see me as I squatted like a praying mantis in aggressive stance with bent arms and a knife in each hand.

The two game rangers had seen Winston leaving me in the afternoon and, when he did not reappear, thought he had been prevented from coming to collect me. Hence their offer to take me back to civilisation. I explained the situation in whispers and they moved off to be swallowed up once again in the darkness of the mangrove belt. It was marvellous to see how quietly and effectively they now worked, and this promised well for the future in Caroni.

During the days that followed I had an opportunity to observe the daily routine of the ibises. It was not possible to distinguish the males from the females since even the calls were the same. One of the parents spent the night on the nest and stayed until about ten o'clock in the morning. The young have two calls. One, like a repeated strumming, is heard either when the chick wants the parents to keep it warm by lying down or to cool it by standing up. The other, a drawn-out warble, is heard when the young demand food. During the morning, food is constantly brought to the nest. The other parent then turns up and mother and father exchange a quick nasal trumpet concert, sometimes accompanied by wing-beating and playful billing. The bird which is relieved from its guard duties flies off to the crab banks, sometimes a long distance away, and the newly arrived parent takes over and in its turn is relieved about four o'clock in the afternoon. The small, hungry chicks with striped bills shake their heads and emit loud shrill begging calls. The bill of the chick points towards a spot at the tip of the adult's bill. If it aims in the right place, the bill moves from the spot, as though travelling along the edge of a bean-pod, up to the base of the bill; the adult opens its bill and the chick's whole head goes into the parent's gullet. A round pellet can be distinctly seen sliding up the red oesophagus and the young one gets its meal—crab with mud sauce! Often the contents are so muddy that the brown Caroni brew runs out over the chick's head and neck. After each meal the remainder of the food slides again slowly down the red neck of the parent, like a snake swallowing medium-sized prey.

There are one, two, or three young in each nest and they grow very fast. During my second period in the tower I was able to follow the progress of one of the chicks up to the time when it was ready to leave the nest. After its first walk around the nest it was only a matter of twenty-four hours before it stepped out, wobbling unsteadily as it tried to keep its balance along a branch. I was terrified it might fall over. It tottered about like a tight-rope walker who pretends to be losing his balance in an effort to get the audience to scream in fright. Here, however, the matter was serious because any young bird that fell off would go down into the muddy water and never survive. I could not give the fledgling any assistance, for to disclose my presence would have enormously increased the danger. However the fledgling passed the test and then moved step by step towards the centre of the tree like all the other ibis chicks.

A mangrove tree, by the way, is a remarkable organism. Thick heavy stems grow downwards like a group of posts, making what appears to be a fine fence in the mud. The peculiarity of the whole thing is explained by the way in which the tree grows. Porous aerial roots as thick as a man's fingers are sent down towards the mud by the first young mangrove bush. There they grow fast, become woody and provide the bush with more nourishment so that it grows in height and sends down still more draperies of aerial roots. Thus there is no limit to the ability of such a tree to spread. The giant in which my tower was hidden covered a circular area with a diameter of about 70 yards and, as I have said, more than three thousand ibises and many more egrets slept there, spread out over the thick canopy of foliage.

The young ibises were fed among the shady layers of the mangrove until fledged, clad in brown and pale grey. The birds do not acquire the scarlet colour until they are sexually mature and, as the plumage changes from dark brown to red, the immature ibis looks as though mud had been spattered over its beautiful red jacket.

It was a wonderful feeling watching the growing numbers of young birds flying in to the roosting tree. They kept together in a couple of large flocks, a few adults showing red amongst them. Strictly speaking this was not a particularly attractive sight but these flocks were the link between the troops of old birds and the legions that I hoped would eventually be hatched in Trinidad in an effectively protected sanctuary. Three years had gone by since the ibis had previously bred and if they had not nested again on the island the whole armada would probably have moved over to Venezuela and perhaps been mown down even more effectively by hunters in the Orinoco delta. Trinidad must save its national bird and I hope that the protection which is still only temporary will acquire the force of law for all time. On the island the birds can build their bridge-head for the invasion of the old haunts along the north and east coast of South America. The population needs a powerful boost—and soon—if it is to survive.

Thus the 'holiday trip' that my wife and I had originally talked about had expanded like a mangrove tree in a way that I could never have envisaged. Over a period of a year there had been one new experience after another. I had done things which had fascinated me ever since I had read about them as a boy, and things which had seemed far beyond my wildest dreams came true. Seeing the oilbirds in the infra-red light of the sniperscope, diving underwater among the thousands of differently coloured forms of life in the Caribbean Sea, taking stock of the army of pink flamingoes or the roseate spoonbills, admiring the easy motion of the anaconda gliding alongside me in the river, watching the egg-laying of the leatherback turtle and the development of the hummingbird chicks into shimmering aviators, all this and much more besides make me full of admiration and wonder for the rich variation in nature. I feel a real sense of contentment at having been privileged to see so much. The nesting of the ibises was one of the highlights of the expedition. It was an intoxication of colour. All attempts to reproduce the red flight in the evening and the unbelievable glow in the plumage must always remain but a pale shadow of reality.

Our world is rich—nature's picture-book gives fantastic views and perspectives both on the past and on the future. Our world is *still* rich, but will we ever understand that the profusion of nature is essential to its very survival? Will our own species, *Homo sapiens*, the thinking man, ever really earn its specific name and stop harrying other species of animal and warring with itself? Is it possible that man's intelligence can eventually be used to create and build up instead of destroying everything that impedes him? Will he be able to prove himself master of his own destiny—or will he continue his lunatic exploitation of nature in the name of progress?

# *Bibliography*

Allen, Glover Morill (1962). *Bats*. New York.

Allen, Robert Porter (1962). *Birds of the Caribbean*. London.

*A new dictionary of birds* (1964). London.

Bent, Arthur Cleveland (1963). *Life Histories of North American Marsh Birds*. New York.

Bond, James (1960). *Birds of the West Indies*. London.

Carr, Archie (1952). *Handbook of Turtles*. New York.

Eibl-Eibesfeldt, I. (1965). *Land of a Thousand Atolls*. London.

Goodwin, George G., and Greenhall, Arthur M. (1961). *A Review of the Bats of Trinidad and Tobago*. (Bulletin of the American Museum of Natural History, Volume 122, Article 3.) New York.

Greenewalt, Crawford H. (1960). *Hummingbirds*. New York.

Greenway, James C. Jr. (1958). *Extinct and Vanishing Birds of the World*. New York.

Griffin, D. R. (1954). Acoustic orientation in the oilbird, *Steatornis*. *Proc. Nat. Acad. Sci.*, 39: 884-93.

(1958). *Listening in the dark*. Yale University Press, New Haven.

Hargreaves, Dorothy and Bob (1960). *Tropical Blossoms of the Caribbean*. Portland, Oregon.

Herklots, G. A. C. (1965). *The Birds of Trinidad and Tobago*. London.

Humboldt, A. von (1817). *Mémoire sur le Guacharo de la caverne de Caripe. Recueil d'observations de zoologie et d'anatomie comparée*. Vol. 2. Paris.

Klingel, Gilbert (1940). *Inagua*. New York.

Meyer de Schauensee, Rodolphe (1964). *The Birds of Colombia.* Narberth, Pennsylvania.

Mitchell, Margaret H. (1957). *Observations on Birds of Southeastern Brazil.* Toronto.

Pope, Clifford H. (1956). *The Reptile World.* London.

(1961). *The Giant Snakes.* New York.

Ruschi, Augusto: Boletim do Museu de Biologia Prof. Mello-Leitão, Santa Teresa—Espírito Santo, Brazil. 3/28.11.1949; 7/28.12.1949; 12/28.9.1953; 30/26.6.1961; 33/16.3.1962.

Santos, Eurico (1955). *Anfíbios e Répteis do Brasil.* Rio de Janeiro.

Schmidt, Karl P., and Inger, Robert F. (1957). *Living Reptiles of the World.* London.

Sibley, C. G. (1960). The electrophoretic patterns of avian eggwhite proteins as taxonomic characters. *Ibis,* 202: 215-59.

Sjögren, Bengt (1963). *Öarna kring vinden.* Halmstad.

*Twentieth Century Bestiary* (1955). New York.

Williams, Eric (1964). *History of the People of Trinidad and Tobago.* London.

Zahl, Paul (1950). Search for the Scarlet Ibis in Venezuela. *National Geographic Magazine,* May 1950: 633-62.

# *Index*

## INDEX OF ANIMALS

## INDEX OF PLACES